WHAT YOUR CHILD WITH ASPERGER'S WANTS YOU TO KNOW

AND HOW YOU CAN HELP THEM

Maja Toudal

Foreword by Tony Attwood

Illustrations by Signe Sønderhousen (Yondoloki)

To my mother and father
who both struggled to understand the needs of an undiagnosed child.
They found a way to help me through life.

ACKNOWLEDGMENTS

There are so many people without whom this book would never have happened, and I feel a need to thank them here.

First and foremost, I want to give my thanks to the many amazing aspies who shared their thoughts and experiences with me, and allowed me to pass on their words through this book. Whether anonymous or named their perspective is vital, and will certainly resonate with many.

I must also express my sincerest gratitude to Dr. Tony Attwood, who gave me the inspiration to begin writing this book, provided detailed comments, endless guidance and immeasurable moral support.

Signe Sønderhousen (Yondoloki), for her beautiful cover and illustrations which bring life and inspiration to the messages I hope to convey.

Anne Skov Jensen, for helping me so much when I felt that time was running out and I didn't know what to do or where to turn.

Sanne and Frederik, for donating their time and skills to help med make a point visual and for making it look cool.

Kirsten, for giving me the confidence to speak my mind.

Pia, for so many painstakingly long hours correcting my grammar.

Christian and Line for the long conversations, their guidance, and invaluable professional input.

Gerd for taking the time to provide comments, and helping me to see this book from an outside perspective.

Even though my mother tongue is Danish and my English may be imperfect I have chosen to write and publish this book in English, to make sure that my words and the words of my fellow aspies who have contributed to this book, can reach a greater audience. I want the reader to know that almost everyone involved in this project, is on the spectrum. Some of the contributors are Danes, like me, and I want to let their words stand as they are because this is their book, as much as it is mine. These are our words to our parents and to parents of children who are like us.

CONTENTS

FOREWORD

Young children who have Asperger's syndrome have great difficulty describing their thoughts, feelings and experiences. They have a different way of perceiving, thinking, learning and relating, and family members and teachers need to know how to accommodate those differences. Eventually, the child may be able to articulate what others need to know. However, that knowledge is already available from mature adults who have the syndrome, such as Maja Toudal.

Maja is able to conceptualize and clearly explain the many aspects of the syndrome, based on her own experiences and on conversations with some of the leading specialists in Autism Spectrum Disorders. She knows what parents need to know.

Asperger's syndrome affects so many aspects of life, hence the wide range of topics covered in this comprehensive book, from making friends to pocket-money. Maja also includes quotations from other adults and adolescents who have Asperger's syndrome, and provides her own wise advice.

Over a number of years, Maja and I have enjoyed many conversations regarding the nature of Asperger's syndrome, and I have absorbed and now incorporate many of her recommendations in my own clinical practice.

This book will become a valued resource at home and in the classroom.

Tony Attwood,
Minds & Hearts Clinic, Brisbane, Australia.

INTRODUCTION

There are so many things I wish I could have told my parents when I was a child, but back then I did not have the words. I could not explain. This, in itself, is one of the important things to know about children with autism spectrum disorders. There is so much going on behind the scenes, but for us, it can be very difficult to hold a thought and express it in words. As I became a teenager and young adult, I saw the benefit in learning to communicate through words. For this project, I have allied myself with adults, young adults and teenagers on the spectrum, as well as specialized professionals, to provide comprehensive and personal insight into our perspective.

In Autism Spectrum Disorders, and hence Asperger's, there are key elements that you must understand in order to work with it. Some professionals may give you one set of rules to remember which revolves around recognizing our areas of difficulties. The rules I am going to list are different in some ways.

I am a human being, no matter how different I seem.

No matter how severely the autism is expressed, no matter how many sensory issues, social impairments, difficulties in executive functions or differences in perception, I am human. This does not make us any less different, but what it does mean is that you should always give me the same amount of respect that you would give to any other.

Non-verbal autistic people are often perceived as intellectually impaired, and they are treated as such. This is unfortunate, because as it turns out, this is far from always the case.

No matter who your child is, you should always assume that any treatment of them as intellectually impaired or disabled, will be perceived by them, and that it will affect their self-worth. This does not mean that they should not be given help, just that it should be given with respect.

Another point to make here, is that it is vital that you get rid of any preconceived notion that autism is something that is "wrong" with your child. We are different, not wrong.

There is something in this world that I am great at.

Sometimes there are so many difficulties in our lives that we, and everyone around us, forget this. But there is something out there that each of us is great at, and not only do we need to find it, we also need the confidence to try it out. And much harder than that, sometimes we also need the conviction and perseverance to keep working on it or to keep doing it, when either we or people around us tell us we are no good. But when we find this ability, whatever it is, and we find out that we are good at it, it becomes a great joy. Perhaps even more so, because we are always (made) so aware of all the abilities we do not have.

I am different from every other person on the spectrum.
I should not have to say this, but many people still assume that each person on the spectrum will have the same traits, same interests, same style of communication etc.

We each have our own personality. This has an effect on how our autism is expressed. We also have different profiles, different expressions and different experiences. Add to this also that each person will have different levels of sensory sensitivity. We are all different, just like you are all different.

Each person with autism is as different to the next as each person without autism is.

I need love.
We may not need it expressed in the same way that you do, but we do still need it. If your child does not like to be touched or hugged, you may perceive that as a rejection. That issue in itself has nothing to do with love from the child's side. (You may also have a child who loves hugs, in which case, I will offer my congratulations.)

Our expression of love can be the smallest things, which you might not connect with the notion of interpersonal love or affection. It can be putting our school bag in our room, or placing it off of the floor because one time you tripped over it. It can be giving you a toy when you are sad, to cheer you up because we know that getting one would make us feel better. It can even be that we make an effort to stay at the dinner table for five minutes longer, because we know that you will prefer it.

No matter what, we need to be loved just as you do. I will suggest that one of the greatest sources for this, may be a pet. This is not to diminish the love that you have for your child, but rather an understanding of how overwhelming human expressions of love can be for your child. Animals are easier to understand, and their emotions much less complicated. Because of this, it may be that a person with ASD may feel more relaxed when there are animals around.

I need space.

Especially from people. Again, this is because humans are so overwhelming to be around, and the only restorative aside from our special interest(s), is solitude.

Always remember always that there is a big difference between being alone, and being lonely. The two are not synonymous for someone with ASD. We can be lonely, but for the most part, being alone is something positive. Please allow us to have this.

I am trying.

Sometimes the people around us get frustrated with all the things we cannot do. Sometimes, they (you) might even think we are just lazy, or not putting enough effort into learning the skills or coping mechanisms we should learn.

I am here to tell you that by far, most people on the spectrum would love to just do all the things we are supposed to, and all the things normal people can do. When you are really ill, for example, when you have a fever, there is nothing you want more than to not have that fever. Well, when autism hinders us in our lives, we wish it did not, as much as anyone around us. We are constantly trying to learn, trying to cope. We just do not always have the capacity to show what is going on, or to truly know what we are even trying to achieve. We just try. We need help, and we are trying.

Sometimes, I need a day off.

And yes, there are days when we just do not want to, just as you have days when the prospect of going to work sucks, or you had days in school when you felt like having a day off from homework.

Well, imagine never having had a day off in your life. Imagine the prospect of never having a day off for the rest of your life, either. Imagine that the only time you can ever relax, is when you are alone. We need to know that we will have time alone soon, preferably scheduled. I realize that saying this to any parent who has children, seems like an insult. Saying this to a parent of a child who has an ASD diagnosis, seems like a slap in the face.

I truly hope, by the time you have read this book, you will understand what I mean when I phrase it the way I do, and that you will understand that it is not meant to diminish everything you do as a parent.
I trust that you will already know that sometimes, everyone needs to take the pressure off. We do, too.

My energy is spent quicker.

This seems silly to say, and may seem like an insult to others on the spectrum, but I have come to realize that when it comes to anything other than our special interest(s), my perceived energy storage, regeneration and capacity, just is not the same as it is for someone who is not autistic. Or perhaps it is not that the capacity is smaller, but that there are so many more things that we have to process, all the time.

Try to picture it as a laptop computer. When you are running on batteries, you will be able to see quite clearly, that if you have 10 programs running, the batteries will drain quicker than if you were only running 2 programs. Now, any person is much the same. If all your sensory and social processing are separate programs that you have to actively open and run and work in, this will drain you more quickly, than if they are automatic programs running in the background.

For computer nerds, this analogy may seem somewhat flawed, but I hope that for the general public, they can overlook any flaws and see the message I am trying to convey.

I need you to catch me, not carry me.
There is a term in Denmark for parents who sweep away the problems their children might face, before they even appear. These are called "curling-parents". From the sport curling, in which the ice is swept in front of the stone, to allow it to travel further and stay straight on its path. This is what not to do. Of course, we need support, though. Everyone needs to know that someone will catch them if they fall, but being there, with your arms stretched out, ready to catch, does not mean holding us down when we try to jump, or lifting us up so we can reach without trying.

In cheerleading, there are people responsible for catching the flyer (the person doing stunts in the air). Of course, they're also responsible for throwing her into in air in the first place, but for the sake of this analogy, we'll ignore that part. No flyer would want to go that high up and do all those dangerous and impressive stunts, without knowing they will arrive safely on the ground. That is your job. You are there to catch us, so we do not get hurt too badly. Never mind a bruise or two, we learn from those, just prevent torn ligaments and broken bones, okay? Probably the most important component in catching rather than carrying, is that you should believe in your child. Believe that they will be okay, that they will learn what they need to, in their own time.

There are so many parents who look at the famous people on the spectrum and say things like; "But that is him/her... my child's autism is much more severe. They will never be able to do that."

The thing is, what you see when you look at those famous individuals is the end result of many years of hard work, of learning skills and applying them. You are not seeing the difficult childhood years when social efforts failed miserably, when they were plagued by feelings of inferiority and even suicidal thoughts. You see the person that came through those struggles.

But when you see your child, right now, you are seeing the hard years. It can be hard to combine the two images and see the possibility that your child can learn amazing skills and can become very successful in life. The fact is, it is possible, and your child needs to believe in this; that they can have a successful and happy future. Because if you do not see it, why and how should they?

Chill out.
I know it is hard. It is much easier said than done. There are many challenges involved in having a child with an autism spectrum disorder, and this is possibly the hardest.

But there is a reason. Your child picks up on your stress, anger and anxiety. All children do this, but we are very sensitive to it because we have no filter. When you are stressed and anxious, we become stressed and anxious, too – we just do not know why. Then we function worse, which gives you another reason (whatever the initial one was) to be stressed and anxious, and then the downward spiral has begun.

If you are calm, if you have hope that everything will be okay, then that is 'contagious', too. If you believe in us, we are given confidence and strength to keep going in life. And the importance of this cannot be understated.

Lastly, before you read this book, I want you to know that I understand that no parent will ever be perfect. If you did everything perfectly the way I describe in the book, taking into account your child's profile and personality, you will still do something wrong. Asking you to do everything I talk about in this book would be asking a human to be superhuman. It cannot be done.

This book is not a guide that should be followed to the letter. It is an attempt at providing you with the inside perspective, so you understand not only what your child might need, but why. It is an attempt at translating and offering advice.

BRIEFLY ABOUT

Before the main chapters, there are some subjects to cover, to give some background knowledge and introduce the ASD way of thinking and perceiving. These will be covered in the following.

YOU

The very first topic I want to address is your side of the family dynamic. I am very aware that much of my advice requires that the rest of the family takes the child with ASD into account first, and leave their own needs for later. No one should reasonably expect you to do this at all times and with all things. That is not what this book is for.

I have heard so many mothers, fathers and siblings expressing worries that they are not doing enough, or that what they are doing is wrong or inadequate and I will tell you the same thing I have told every single one of them: You cannot take care of your child if you have not taken care of yourself. You need to be okay with you. You need to find, first and foremost, a way to relieve your stress, to relax, to get the sleep you need and have something good to eat. You need to schedule time for your own hobby, a night to read quietly or a cheerful lunch with a friend because if you neglect yourself you will have nothing left to give. So in effect, your child needs you to be okay, too.

And the rest of the family needs to be okay. They need time to do the things they love or for relaxing because otherwise you will end up with a problem in your family dynamics; a culture in which the person with ASD makes the rules and sets the schedule for everyone, and ultimately this is not beneficial to anyone.

Due to the issues it can cause when the rest of the family is, in a sense, sacrificed to meet the needs of the ASD person, I want to include, very specifically, the point that the suggestions and advice in this book are meant precisely as suggestions, and that there is no expectation that all of them will be implemented. You need to find the compromises that work in your family in order to make room for every family member, so far as such compromises are possible.

You, your spouse and any additional children are every bit as important family members as the child with ASD is, and none of you should be expected to give up everything in an effort to meet impossible standards, such as would be set by this book, if one attempted to do everything. Please, take care of you, too.

CHANGES TO DIAGNOSTIC CRITERIA (DSM-5)

In 2013, The Diagnostic and Statistical Manual of Mental Disorders 4th edition (DSM) was updated to the latest 5th edition. In this new edition, Autism, Infantile Autism, Asperger's Syndrome and several other diagnoses were all lumped into the new diagnosis Autism Spectrum Disorder. In this, there are three specified 'levels' of ASD, of which 1 is the mildest and 3 is the most severe.

This is not really news at all, since Professionals recognized the previous diagnoses as being related under the term Autism Spectrum Disorder (or Autism Spectrum Condition, which is the term many of those with the diagnoses prefer). However, the new criteria do make it harder for some to get a clinical diagnosis where previously they would have gotten one.

The DSM is written by the American Psychiatric Association, and some countries still use completely different diagnostic manuals, so depending on which country you live in, Asperger's, Infantile Autism etc., may still be current diagnoses. This means that in the global community, there is now some confusion as to whether or not Asperger's is a 'real' diagnosis or not. There are many who have received this diagnosis in the past, and many more will in the countries that do not go by the DSM. And as we already knew that Asperger's was a part of the spectrum, I do not see the diagnoses as separate at all. Basically, Asperger's has simply changed its name to 'ASD-1'.

The reason I still use the term Asperger's, as well as the terms Autism and ASD, is because they are all a part of the same spectrum. There is a lot of research regarding Asperger's which is still valid, and there is a significant amount of literature out there on the topic. Therefore, for simplicity and continuity, my use of the terms remains unchanged.

It seems the right time clarify here that in this book, I use the terms person with ASD and aspie (person with Asperger's) interchangeably. This doesn't mean that they always are, nor that it is scientifically correct, but for the purposes of this book, they will be synonymous.

AMYGDALA AND EMOTIONS

Studies have shown that people on the autistic spectrum have differences in the amygdala. This part of the brain has to do with the recognition and regulation of emotions. The difference we have means that comparatively, we have difficulties with regulating our emotions, perceiving the emotions of ourselves and others, as well as regulating our reactions to these emotions.

The difficulty in regulating our emotions shows in the lack of nuances. It is not universal, of course, but people on the spectrum tend to feel in neutrals and extremes. If we picture the range of an emotion of a scale of 0-10, 0 being neutral, then the average person will spend very little time in the 8-10 range of any emotion. Those levels are triggered only by traumatic or otherwise big events, such as being cheated on, losing a steady income or a death in the family, and on the scale of happiness it might be getting a hard earned promotion, being proposed to, becoming a parent etc.

People on the autistic spectrum can feel great levels of frustration or despair if we are 5 minutes late for school or forgot our pencil-case at home. Likewise, we can feel extreme happiness at getting a perfect score on a spelling test or finding an extra item for our collection (which is a special interest of many of us).

We can also have a surprisingly neutral reaction to some things. Importantly, the things we do or do not react to depend on the person: what is and is not important to them at this time. The result is that while the average person spends most time in the 0-5 range, and it takes a lot for them to go above 7, people on the autistic spectrum spend most time between 0-2 and 8-10. It is quite possible to be in between, as it is possible for someone non ASD (in this book, people who do not have ASD are often referred to as neurotypical or NT, a term used to refer to people with typical neurological behavior and development) to be at 8-10, but this is an indicator of how our emotional life generally is.

The trouble with this is that especially as children, we will have a tendency to skip everything between 2 and 8. If we, as mentioned in the earlier example, forget our pencil-case, we go to school feeling fairly content, say happy at a 1, then the moment when we realize that our pencil-case is not in the school bag, a child with ASD may very well go straight from happy 1, to despair 9.

"Life tends to be either 'happy' or 'not happy', 'angry' or 'not angry'. All the 'in between' emotions on the continuum get missed. I jump from calm to panic in one major step." (Lawson 2001, p.119)

This is quite frustrating for the person with ASD, as well as for those around us. As you can probably imagine, being at negative emotional extremes is not pleasant, and once we develop the ability to realize that others do not respond well to these emotional outbursts, it will make us embarrassed, and we will often become afraid of being in situations that may cause extreme emotions, because we want to avoid the shame and embarrassment. This tendency for our emotional life to be experienced in extremes will influence much of the advice in this book.

COGNITIVE ABILITIES

This term refers to thinking and learning abilities. In people without ASD, these skills are usually quite balanced. But this is not the case in people with ASD. Our cognitive ability profile can be extremely unbalanced.

We may be able to teach ourselves to read, spell and solve mathematical problems, but at the same time not have the ability to find our way around the school.

There is a tendency to have a one track mind and not being able to steer off a particular course of thinking, even after we have realized it is wrong, and there is also usually a great fear of mistakes. On top of this, there is a tendency toward attention problems at school – many of which have to do with our focus on detail and inability to control this – as well as problems in executive functioning (which has to do with organization and planning, working memory, impulse control, time management, prioritizing, understanding abstract concepts etc. Think of it as the CEO in our brains being a scatterbrained and disorganized person, and you have the general idea). One girl expressed one way in which her problems in executive functioning reveal themselves:

"It's easy doing things when I'm already doing them, but what is difficult is getting started and finishing tasks. I find it extremely frustrating and I've spoken to many psychologists and other professionals about it, trying to find solutions." (Anonymous personal communication.)

There are many fancy words that cover our problems and discrepancies in our cognitive abilities, but what I honestly need you to take away from this is that your child's ability to think and learn in different situations and with regard to different academic and life skills, will possibly be very unbalanced. And you may become very frustrated at times, thinking: "Why can he/she not do this, when he/she is so smart!?" So I want you to know, that whatever we are good and not so good at are probably not connected, and you should expect very different learning curves.

Your child might be able to read and understand books that are several grades ahead, but not be able to put their t-shirt on the right way. Likewise, they may be able to draw or paint the most incredible and photorealistic art, but not be able to grasp the difference between five minutes and an hour.

As one of the most famous people with autism, Temple Grandin, describes in one of her books:

"My mind is completely visual and spatial work such as drawing is easy. I taught myself drafting in six months. I have designed big steel and concrete cattle facilities, but

17

remembering a phone number or adding up numbers in my head is still difficult. I have to write them down. Every piece of information I have memorized is visual." (Grandin 1984, p.145)

Our thinking and learning abilities are very unpredictable, and may also change very suddenly, especially due to maturity, hormonal changes and/or traumatic events.

You will be frustrated, and you will probably never completely understand why they can do one thing but not another. That is okay. We also feel frustrated about this, perhaps even more so at times. However, it is a part of being a person on the autistic spectrum.

CO-MORBIDITY

This refers simply to one or more additional diagnoses co-occurring with the primary one. There are many different diagnoses one might have, while also having ASD. Some of the most common ones are ADHD (Attention Deficit Hyperactivity Disorder), anxiety, depression and OCD (Obsessive Compulsive Disorder).

It is always a challenge to combine ASD with a life in a society which is not made for people like us, but extra diagnoses make it quite difficult at times.

It is important to remember that ASD changes the way you perceive the world, and any additional diagnosis is also changed by ASD. The way it is expressed, and the way it should be treated. This is why it is important to make sure that the people involved in treating your child have specialized education in ASD.

It is also very important to understand where one diagnosis ends and the other begins, and how they overlap. So your job in educating yourself has not only doubled with each additional diagnosis, but ever so slightly more.

The most important part is, of course, to make sure that you are not learning the theory of how the diagnoses should interact, but instead how they do interact in exactly your child. Your child's ASD profile (including the severity or level) has a great deal to say in how they might be affected by for example, anxiety. How severe the anxiety is, adds yet another dynamic to consider. Your child also needs to learn these things as they grow up and get older, as having a greater understanding of their profile and diagnoses will increase their ability to create a happy and fulfilling life for themselves.

It is very difficult to know yourself well enough to know which of your diagnoses just happens to be the primary one affecting you right now so it will be even more difficult for you to know it for your child. It is not easy for them to learn, yet if they can, it will help them significantly. So it is a good place to put in some extra effort.

EMPATHY AND SYMPATHY

First I will have to define these words, so as to make sure my meaning comes through correctly. So here are the definitions I am working with:

Empathy: the ability to share and understand the feelings of another.

Sympathy: feelings of compassion and sorrow for someone else's misfortune.

There are then two parts to having empathy, one is to share an emotion; another is to understand an emotion. Having sympathy is a seemingly simpler matter, in that the concept deals with whether you feel compassion or not.

It is said by some that people with ASD do not have empathy. This is not entirely true. Our problem is not always that we do not know when you are in pain, but rather that we cannot cope with the emotion – it is too big and it hurts – and also because we do not necessarily know where the emotion comes from. We do not know the why. So we both do and do not have empathy.

However, this does not mean that we are awful people who do not care. Because while we do not know why you are in pain, and we are afraid of doing the wrong thing when trying to "fix it", we certainly do not want you to be in pain. In short, we can have problems with empathy, or certain parts of it, but we do have sympathy.

In Tony Attwood's book "The Complete Guide to Asperger's Syndrome", he remarks on a quote from Nita Jackson, in which she describes making one of the types of mistakes which might make it seem that we lack sympathy:

"I discovered that I couldn't comprehend people's facial expressions, what they said or the way in which they said it. Reminiscing on my early school days I realized how I used to laugh when someone cried because I thought the other person was laughing. I can't understand how I made this mistake – all I know is that I did this often." (N. Jackson 2002, p.20)

Dr. Attwood notes on this example that: "The extreme facial expressions for someone crying and laughing can be very similar. Both emotions can produce tears. The confusion for someone with Asperger's syndrome is quite understandable but can be misinterpreted by others." (Attwood 2007, p.153)

So a misunderstanding occurs twice in such a situation. First, we misread crying as laughing, which makes us laugh "with" this other person. The person who is crying and other onlookers then assume that we know that the person is, in fact, crying, not laughing, and so they will judge our laughter as cruelty.

It is important to always remember that when you see your child (or someone else you know, who has ASD) not giving the correct response to an emotion, that they are not cold and uncaring, but rather, it is likely that they either shut down because the emotion is too overwhelming for them to cope with, or that they do not know the correct way to respond, and either misinterpreted the situation or choose to do nothing out of fear of making a mistake.

In connection with the differences we have with regard to emotions (see Amygdala and Emotions), this can give some issues with empathy, in the sense that it is hard for us to relate to an emotion we have never felt.

If we put emotions on a scale from 1-10, where 1 is quite neutral and 10 is extreme, we can explore this in relatively simple terms. If you are angry at level 6, but I have only ever experienced angry at 1-2 or 9-10, then I do not know what 6 feels like.

When I get older and I learn to recognize the in-between emotions, I may suddenly relate emotionally to events that happened many years ago, but as a child, it is very difficult. Keep this in mind when discussing emotions with your child.

A good tool to use for communication regarding emotions and the scale of them, is the CAT-Kit, developed by Kirsten Callesen and Tony Attwood. You can find this online at cat-kit.com.

HOW TO GIVE ADVICE

The first thing is that there is no way to guarantee the desired result. I cannot promise you that anything I write here will be spot on.

Encourage asking for help to solve problems. This is the best thing in the long term, because once we learn that it is okay to ask for help, and getting help does not mean we are stupid, then we will be more receptive to help and advice in general.

Be careful of criticism. Make it either neutral or positive. Be like a GPS; keep emotions out and focus on the task. If you go a different way than the GPS suggests, it will not yell or get angry, and it will not criticize your driving skills, it will simply calculate a new route and tell you the new instructions.

Stay away from "You are not doing it right" and "Can't you see...?" and try adapting your language into "I think others have maybe had the same problem maybe someone has already found a solution. We can try searching online?" Of course, when dealing with homework, searching online for answers might not be the way to go. Be careful of "butting in" and forcing help and advice on your child. If they are still in the "I can figure it out myself!"-mode, then they are not likely to be happy to accept advice. This can be very hard, I realize, but it is important. Additionally, it can help the process of teaching your child to ask for help, because they will not have the experience that help is something others force on you, but something you choose to ask for when you need it.

Offer knowledge, but do not act superior. To explain this properly, I will include a widely shared experience amongst those of us with ASD.

In school, there is usually at least one teacher we do not like. We do not always understand, while we are young, why this particular teacher makes us extra stubborn or irritable, but they do. Adults may say: "Maybe it is because of the subject they teach?" and they may very well be right in some cases. But for many of us, looking back, we realize the reason was, actually, that the teacher acted superior.

"I respond much better when people speak to me as an equal. It is very important that I feel safe and comfortable with the people who give me advice or teach me. If I feel safer and have more respect for the teachers, it is easier for me to focus. I also feel less inclined to be overly skeptical of what they tell me, or to challenge their authority." (Anonymous, personal communication.)

Children with ASD react very badly to being spoken down to, being patronized. An attitude of "I am an adult, so I know better" or "I am smarter than you" (note, not just saying this, but the attitude of it!), will be picked up by the child, and met with resistance.

LANGUAGE

There are several parts to the language differences between those on the spectrum and those not. It will be easiest, I think, to describe these separately, although these are not entirely separate issues.

We understand the meaning of a word, not the connotation – which is a learned ability. It can be learned, but it takes time. We use the word in the meaning we understand it to have. This is not necessarily the dictionary definition, though in many cases it will be – even in cases of long, academic words that a child would usually not know, it is not uncommon for children with ASD to have exceptional and advanced vocabularies, especially when it pertains to a special interest.

This then means that we use language in a very literal way, and understand it in a literal way. Some do this much more than others, and again, as we get older, this can change. But as children it means that especially metaphors and sarcasm can be difficult, and simple instructions or rules can be misunderstood, often because they are not generalized, as described by Donna Williams:

"The significance of what people said to me, when it sank in as more than just words, was always taken to apply only to that particular moment or situation. Thus, when I once received a serious lecture about writing graffiti on Parliament House during an excursion, I agreed that I'd never do this again and then, ten minutes later, was caught outside writing different graffiti on the school wall. To me, I was not ignoring what they said, nor was I trying to be funny: I had not done exactly the same thing as I had done before." (Williams 1998, p.64)

In some cases, we may view language simply as a tool to communicate messages and ideas, but not so much emotions and social relations. This understanding of language usually comes without the appropriate connotations, and also without understanding the history of certain words or phrases, which means we may sometimes say something very inappropriate, but have absolutely no idea why. It also means we may say something that sounds like a joke to others without realizing why they perceive it as funny.

We do not notice the body language and tone of voice you use to regulate meaning to the same degree or amount of detail (or alternatively, we notice too many details and therefore teach ourselves to ignore them, due to the amount of effort it takes to dissect and translate each detail).

In my opinion, this is the basis of a great deal of the misunderstandings that occur when neurotypicals and people with ASD communicate.

As shown in this model, the neurotypical (NT) approaches a conversation with not only words, but also their connotations with the (to them) appropriate body language, facial mimicry and vocal intonation, and they expect to see these reflected in the person they speak to. The person with ASD (AS) expects all the important information to be in the words themselves and may not even be able to read everything else yet, either due to age and not having learnt yet, or not being capable of learning (this part is individual).

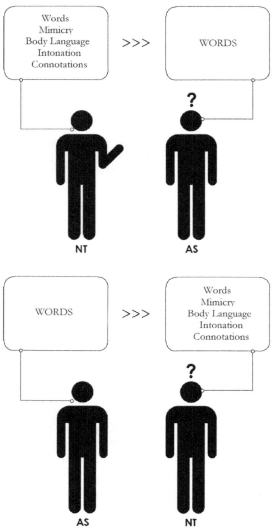

This means that the person with ASD misses a lot of information coming from the neurotypical, but just as importantly, the neurotypical expects the person with ASD to use body language etc. in their communication and interprets the communication accordingly – that is, they are interpreting the lack of body language etc. to carry meaning in the same way that the presence of it would have in their own communication. With missing information on one side, and assumed information on the other, a great number of misunderstandings can occur in everyday life. Not only between strangers, but also between people who otherwise know each other, because occasionally, each side will forget their respective handicap in communicating with the other party.

What does this mean?

Firstly, it means we need to learn the concept of these things to the degree that we can cope with it. It takes time, but it makes life easier later on.

Secondly, it means that you should not expect us to know any of this and much less be able to act accordingly. Try as much as possible to use words that convey the full meaning of what you mean to say.

Thirdly, never attribute added or hidden meaning to anything we say. We may get emotional and say emotional things that do not convey how we feel when calm, but we do not manipulate, we do not hide behind misleading statements.

This also means that if you ask "How are you feeling?" you will get the true answer. We will not say "fine" unless we know that this is the expected response. We will tell you how we actually feel – if we know, of course.

Disclaimer: While comparatively rare, some people in the "high functioning" end of the spectrum can and do learn to lie, especially in cases where it avoids confrontation to do so. Some can also learn crude methods of manipulation or ways of avoiding certain situations.

LOSS OF SKILLS

A frustrating and unfortunately consistent problem for many people on the autistic spectrum is loss of skills. Previously mastered skills may be lost after experiencing trauma or long term stress. Examples of skills that may be lost are: Tying shoelaces, reading or even speaking. It is important to remember that the skill is actually lost, and that we are not simply refusing to do these things though to an outsider it may appear so. They have truly lost that skill and must re-learn it, just as they had to learn it the first time.

This can be extraordinarily frustrating and scary to the person who suddenly loses one or several skills, but also to people around them. A part of the frightening aspect is that it is completely unfamiliar; it is not something one usually sees or hears of, but another part is that it can make everyone nervous as to what other skills might be lost. This is a legitimate concern, but the primary concern should be in preventing future trauma, as that in turn will help to prevent future loss of skills.

Some of the skills we are prone to losing are social skills and motor skills. If this happens, I recommend focusing first on decreasing any anxiety or depression that may result from the loss of skills, before moving on to re-learning the skill, as re-learning a skill is usually expressed as being very taxing and at times feeling humiliating; because of course, the person recalls having this skill, but simply cannot remember how to do it.

My advice is to avoid re-traumatizing the person though creating a mood dominated by anxiety with regard to further loss of skills: Do your best not to treat it as a big deal. Rather, this is a fact of life and one must move on and re-learn the lost skills at the pace at which this is reasonable, and as always, please consult a professional whenever in doubt.

It is also possible to have a temporary loss of skill where, typically in a very stressful situation, we may lose the ability to speak, for example. Once we calm back down the skill returns. This issue seems to have more to do with short term stress, related to our tendency to react in emotional extremes. Once again, do contact a professional about this as it can become a real issue in life.

PROFILES

In Autism Spectrum Disorders, we often refer to someone's profile. It really just means "how autism is expressed in this particular person". You will have an idea of it just from knowing them.

The concept of autistic profiles was introduced after professionals discovered how individual autism was, and especially after general gender differences were discovered.

I will give a quick introduction to the general, classic "male" and "female" profiles. I put these in quotation marks, because while they mostly apply to the genders of boy and girl, they are by no means absolute. Girls can have the male or classic profile, so called because those were the traits first discovered and described, and likewise, boys can have the female profile.

The classic profile describes someone who has little to no interest in social interactions, or seemingly so, or who is socially intrusive and intense to a degree that is uncomfortable for others. Often, it is not mentioned that someone can change back and forth between these two ways of acting, often depending on the company, or shifts in their overall emotional state – for example, someone who has previously been socially motivated can become withdrawn and introverted during stressful periods, after a traumatic experience or due to depression. They are described as having relatively few conventionally expressed emotions, often using either little to no facial expressions, or alternatively extreme ones that are or can seem forced, for example, a smile may look like a grimace rather than a genuine smile. Classic autism/ASD is also marked by having physical, externalized meltdowns, having very few friends at any stage of life, and having a special interest that is unusual both in focus and degree.

Social skills can be learned slowly and consciously, need thorough rehearsed, and are non-adaptable, meaning they will only be applied to the particular rehearsed situation, and not transferred to similar situations.

The IQ and cognitive abilities profile are distinguished by being uneven (meaning they can be very high in one or several categories, but very low in others – where neurotypical people are relatively even), which is why some people may be able to study astrophysics at a young age, but never learn to tie their own shoes.

The female profile is very different, though the underlying neurological differences from the norm are the same as in the classic profile. It describes someone who is more interested in socializing, but whose abilities are superficial when no guide is available. There is a tendency to mimic or copy the behavior of others, even going as far as copying someone else's accent, appearance, mannerisms and interests. There can be different reasons for this, and usually, the copying behavior is most apparent in the childhood years, with more adaptable social skills being learned through the teenage and adult years. They will tend to have more friends than those with the classic profile – though still not as many as a neurotypical peer.

Facial expressions, gestures and vocal intonation will be closer to the norm, and the emotional range as well appears more "normal" though it usually is not. Rather, someone with the female profile is more likely to hide extreme emotional reactions and "save them" for later.

Due to the work they put into socializing and controlling expressions etc., people with this profile will have a huge expense of energy in analyzing and coping with the social world. All people with ASD spend a lot of energy on this, some individuals with this profile just spend even more. Meltdowns are more likely to be internalized, and there can be a higher tendency towards depressions, self-harm, anxiety, eating disorders and low confidence, though these are issues for a great number of those with ASD.

For those with the female profile, it is likely that a special interest will have a focus that is "normal" or more socially acceptable than what is associated with the classic profile, but that the degree of interest in the topic is unusual. For example, she may like Barbies or boybands the same as her neurotypical peers, but her knowledge on the topic is extreme in comparison. She may have the same amount of posters of horses as her neurotypical friend, but her knowledge on the topic is extreme in comparison. Instead of merely knowing the breeds, she may also be able to tell you which edition of which magazine each poster came from, and the history of the breed, the physiological facts that differ between them, and so on and so forth.

As with the classic profile, there is an unbalanced IQ profile and cognitive abilities profile attached. However, since many of the girls are very concerned with appearing normal, they may work extremely hard to cover up the things they are not good at, especially if they are noticeable things like not being able to tie their shoes. They may also only cover them up at school and with other family members, but not care to hide it from you.

This is a quick introduction, and therefore not complete. The point of this section is not to give you a recipe for what to expect, but rather, to give you an idea of what professionals expect and can possibly misunderstand – as the classic profile is still the most widely known and thus the female profile is often misinterpreted or dismissed – and much more importantly, to give you an idea of the wide range of profiles within Autism Spectrum Disorders.

Do not expect your child to have one or the other profile. They will not. They will have their own unique profile.

SENSORY SENSITIVITIES

Dr. Tony Attwood uses an explanation of the capacity for social interaction that I find extremely useful as the foundation to describe sensory sensitivities. He invites us to imagine the brain as a clearing in a forest. In the center, there will be a plant that represents the social part of the brain. For a person who is not on the autistic spectrum, this plant is a tree. It grows strong and tall, and its branches and leaves take up a lot of space, blocking sunlight from the plants underneath. It uses most of the water and nutrients from the soil. All of this means that the other plants – the parts of the brain that are dedicated to senses – remain small flowers.

The non-ASD brain sacrifices other aspects to feed the social one.

But for a person with ASD, the social plant is a small tree, a bush or even just a flower. It does not keep sunlight, water or nutrients from the other plants, allowing them to grow bigger and stronger. Therefore, people with ASD have all kinds of sensory sensitivities. They can be auditory (especially sudden or 'sharp' noises, and pitch), tactile, visual, aroma, proprioceptive (position and movement of the body), pain (either hyper-sensitivity or hypo-sensitivity, in which pain is not felt as strongly or not at all), temperature sensitivities (again, either hyper- or hypo-sensitivity), and there can also be a mind and body connection issue – which can stem from the same sort of neurological reasons as sensory sensitivities, or it can be a psychological issue in which case it will usually appear after a traumatic event.

A person with ASD can have only one sense that is a lot stronger (or weaker) or they can have several. This means that we experience certain things differently. A taste, smell or texture that is perfectly fine for you may assault our senses. Light changing or vibrating may be a relatively mild annoyance for you, or you may be completely able to discard it, but it is so overwhelming for us that we are unable to move forward until it has been processed (which, in the case of sensory experiences like vibrating light, we may not be able to at all).

We all have different sensory sensitivities. The sensory profile is unique to the person, and can change over time. Certain things can get better or worse with age or with environmental changes and most often extreme emotional states such as depression, anxiety and stress can mean that we have so little energy left to process the sensory experiences that our whole world seems to collapse.

Coping strategies can be learned, but in times of emotional stress, we may not be able to use them. Remember that your child is not making it up or being purposefully difficult. It torments them just as much as it does you, if not more. Every person experiences sensory sensitivities in their own way, and for that reason it is hard to give one clear description of it. A quote from Carolyn, a woman with Asperger's syndrome, published in The Complete Guide to Asperger's Syndrome by Tony Attwood, gives one example:

"With fluorescent lights it's not only the glare that gets me, it's the flicker as well. It produces 'shadows' in my vision (which were very scary when I was young) and long exposure can lead to confusion and dizziness often resulting in migraine." (email to Tony.)

One aspect that is rarely spoken of when describing sensory sensitivities is that there are also positive sensitivities. For example, there can be certain textures or sounds that we enjoy to such an extent that it can stabilize our moods or even distract us from stressful elements in our surroundings. Most of these are probably unnoticed by those around us, yet not all, as can be seen in the case of Donna Williams. She describes a positive sensory sensitivity in her book "Nobody Nowhere":

"One sound, however, which I loved to hear was the sound of anything metal. Unfortunately for my mother, our doorbell fell into this category, and I spent ages obsessively ringing it." (Williams 1998, p.45)

If your child has such a positive reaction to for example a food item, the smell of a particular fabric softener or flower, harmonic sound, a certain color or pattern, it can be very useful to encourage using it as a coping mechanism, and finding ways to use it as positive reinforcement, especially in the early years.

Not everyone has a strongly positive sensory sensitivity, and not everyone has distinct sensory sensitivities. As with everything else on the spectrum, it is unique to the individual. Find out what your child's profile is, and keep track if there are important changes. You can use it to avoid the bad sensory experiences and grant extra access to the good ones. Lastly, people with ASD are more prone to a phenomenon called synesthesia. This is when sensory input triggers a perception in a second sense. The most common is when a written word or symbol triggers a color or sound-color, but it may be different things. So if you discover that your child has this, do not be alarmed. It is a known phenomenon, and it is, as far as we know, simply the 'wiring' in the brain that connects the senses in a way that is relatively uncommon. People without ASD can have this, too, but are less prone to it.

THEORY OF MIND AND SOCIAL REASONING

Theory of mind is a term that is used in describing how good or bad someone is at determining why other people do what they do, how they think, etc., and using this to predict behavior. In short – how good is my theory of your mind compared to someone whose theory is average? The term also includes 'theory of one's own mind', meaning: how well do I understand my own mind, the reasons behind my own actions and decisions etc.

In people with ASD, the theory of mind skills (ToM) are decreased and delayed. These skills can be learned, however. For neurotypicals, these skills develop in early childhood, and they do so intuitively. Generally, people develop these skills at a certain rate, such that you can say that by age this or that, a neurotypical child should be able to do this or that. There is a test called "The Sally – Anne test" which can be used very efficiently at certain ages to establish the difference between a neurotypical child's ToM skills and those of a child with ASD. What the test will generally show, is that a child with ASD has a tendency to believe that others share their knowledge and understanding of the world, rather than possessing their own, based on separate experiences. This is what it means to lack Theory of Mind skills.

As mentioned, our skills in this area can increase, we can learn a great deal, but the progression and natural learning of these skills will be, to one extent or another, delayed, and without making a continued effort to learn said skills, we will not reach a similar understanding of this social skill as a neurotypical person, even in adulthood. Ellen, a teenage girl with ASD describes:

"I think I was 12 or 13 before I realized that people's thoughts and reasoning were different from my own. I understood that people were different from me (we did not look the same, we acted differently etc.) but I always assumed that their thinking was the same as mine. That they'd find a joke funny because I did, that they'd like my favorite band (because it was most definitely the best music ever) and that they would come to the same conclusions as me. I had not even considered that others' minds did not work the same way as mine before I got my diagnosis." (Ellen, personal communication.)

We will tend to describe actions much more than thoughts, feelings and intentions, which means that our understanding of situations and people lacks an element, and this is not only very frustrating for everyone close to us, it is also very frustrating for us. However – our 'learned' theory of mind skills can reach quite advanced levels, especially when receiving help in learning them, and learning to pass a test like the Sally-Anne test, can in most cases be accomplished at a rate that is not much delayed from the norm.

Once we learn the trick to ToM, we can learn on our own as well. Processing time in ToM tasks will generally still be greater than that of a neurotypical person, even though we can learn to reach the proper conclusions about others' thoughts, feelings and intentions, at least more often than otherwise.

Social reasoning skills and theory of mind skills are also decreased in stressful situations, so the more people and the more sources of sound etc. there are, the worse our skills will be. So allow us some calm and some time, and make sure that in helping us learn these skills, you respect our intelligence. We learn better when we feel smart, just as you do.

SOCIAL "LANGUAGES"

I am often asked why I think people with ASD should learn some adaptive skills, in terms of communicating with the "neurotypical" world. There is a short answer, and a much longer explanation for that answer.

The short answer is: It is beneficial to any person to learn to communicate with others to the best of their ability because it helps them get what they need to survive and thrive in the long run.

Here is the explanation:
The neurotypical/non-autistic person uses (seemingly by instinct) all sorts of cues in their communication, such as connotations, vocal intonation, body language and so on. The child (or even adult) with ASD uses words primarily and if we take note of the rest, it is secondary to the words. These different ways of engaging socially result in a lot of misunderstandings.

This is where an analogy of languages may be useful. I personally speak only two languages fluently; Danish and English. Danish is a language only spoken by approximately 5-6 million people in the world, whereas English is spoken by several hundred million people. So when I travel the world, the odds of my meeting someone who speaks English are far greater than meeting someone who speaks Danish. Because of this, it is very helpful for me to be able to speak English, and the better I do so, the easier it will be for me to navigate the countries in which English is the national language, as well as the countries where it is a second language, and where Danish is not spoken at all.

In much the same way that I speak different languages I also speak "aspie" and "NT" which makes life a lot easier. There are comparatively few aspies/people with ASD, so being able to speak "NT" makes my life easier. It does not matter if my "NT" skill only goes far enough for me to communicate the concepts of "Hi", "Help" and "Thank you", the skill is still useful. Likewise, it is useful for a neurotypical person, if they know someone who has ASD, to be able to speak "aspie". That way, communication is made easier.

Neither of us have to change who we are in order to communicate better, we only have to learn to translate what we mean. Your child does not have to be someone different in order to learn to speak "NT", but rather, they simply learn some skills to translate who they are, in a manner that more people may understand. This way, they are more likely to get their point across, and less likely to be misunderstood in negative ways.

Try thinking of the ASD way of communicating as a separate language or culture, and teach us to navigate the "NT" world as you would teach us to navigate any other culture.

STIMMING

It is very common to come across this term when navigating the world of information about autism, but for the most part, what you get is a sterile and factual description of what it is: self-stimulatory behavior such as flapping, rocking, spinning, or repetition of sounds, words or phrases. It is most often a symptom of autism, but can also be seen in individuals who are not on the spectrum.

What you are less likely to hear is why we do it, how common it actually is, and what it is like.

The sort of stimming associated with autism is usually very obvious to observers. It is either loud or big in some way. But many very common behaviors have the same functions for everyone else that our forms of stimming have for us. It can be a way to try to control emotional response, as a girl with Asperger's describes:

"I stim when I can feel myself getting sad or angry, to try to stop my emotion from getting too big. I do it to try to control the feeling. It does not always work, especially when someone says something to me that aggravates the emotion." (Anonymous, personal communication.)

Another girl expressed that stimming is necessary for her to cope with the world in general:

"I think I would explode if I weren't allowed to stim. It's like scratching an itch or sneezing. I can't help it and — for me at least — it feels completely natural. I'm a very anxious and sensitive person, and with the world being crazy and overwhelming, stimming helps me cope." (Ellen, personal communication.)

It can also be a way to block unwanted sensory input, by substituting our own, more pleasing (to us), and more predictable output. Frequently, this is done by putting our hands over our ears, humming or otherwise making noise, or perhaps rocking or hitting/tapping something with our hands. The more physically extreme the stim, the less bearable the unwanted sensory input is likely to be.

I should note here that some of the generalizations I make in this book may not necessarily be applicable to more severe cases of autism. I do not wish to speak on their behalf where I cannot.

With regard to the subject of stimming, what I mean to say is that those who can regulate which stimming method to use, will to the best of their ability use the less violent/large or loud physical methods when they are sufficient. Meaning; if it is possible to distract myself from or override the unwanted sensory input by tapping my fingers together or squeezing an object in my hand, then I will not likely begin to hit my forehead or anything of that sort. I go through the possibilities starting with the most benign and less painful, and when one "level" of stimming fails to do its job, I move on to the next.

Unfortunately, not everyone has the control or understanding of their own stimming to consciously apply them as a tool, and they may only know a few ways to attempt to override the unwanted input, or it may even sometimes be impossible. As certain stimuli are physically and emotionally unbearable for us, this is when breakdowns often occur.

An example of sensory stimuli that is hard to bear even for people who are not on the spectrum could perhaps be having your teeth worked on at the dentist's. How do you cope? Do you perhaps try to think of a "happy place" or try to remember a song in your mind to distract yourself? You may even grip the arms of the chair really hard with your hands, or squeeze your eyes shut? So, what sorts of common behaviors are forms of stimming? Tapping your foot when anxious is an avenue for keeping that emotion in check. Similarly, biting your nails or pacing could also easily be seen as "emotional" stimming. So really, the big differences lie in whether or not you have sensory sensitivities to deal with, and also, the quantity and form of stimming. We do it more often and more obviously.

It can be debated whether or not there might be a category of stimming which purely concerns creating pleasant sensory input. We can become very addicted to repetitively causing some form of sensory experience, which we find pleasurable. Touching a certain fabric or hearing specific sounds, for example.

I might be reluctant to call it a stim because the word stimming is associated with regulating our responses to negative emotions or sensory input, and these would go beyond that definition. However, I am inclined to call these activities "stimming" because they can in many cases be used very efficiently to regulate negative emotions or sensory input, sometimes much more so than any previously discovered version of stimming.

One category these almost always fall into, is pleasant sensory "sensitivities".

WHAT I WANT YOU TO KNOW ABOUT

While reading the main chapters, I recommend that you keep the introduction in mind, as well as to refer back to any "Briefly About" that I mention, should you not previously have read it.

FOOD AND DINNERTIME

Because such a large proportion of people with ASD have sensory sensitivities with regard to the taste, smell and texture of food, this is one of the earliest problems many run into. And even if there does not seem to be any significant sensory sensitivities in this area, the social aspects will often show themselves, either at home or at school.

Sensory Sensitivity

One of the first things that many parents of children on the autistic spectrum will experience is the child's sensory sensitivity. Each child is different and so is their sensory profile. Attempting to explain sensory sensitivity to those who have never dealt with it as a real problem is tricky but I think perhaps food is a good place to start.

Almost everyone has a type of food they do not like. Some do not like a specific kind of soup or shellfish or vegetable. Others do not like a specific type of meat or perhaps even a specific piece of an animal such as liver and tongue. Whatever it may be, try to picture the type of food you dislike the most. Imagine how it looks, how it tastes, how it smells and how it feels in your mouth. Ask yourself why you dislike it. Is it one element or several? Which ones? The difference between you and your child is that for them, it is likely not just one or two things they dislike to eat, it can be a whole variety of things, all perhaps for different reasons.

For young children, the problem is the inability to explain why they do not want to eat this food and parents can become frustrated with the limited diet of their child and attempt to force them to eat new things. This might work if your child is neurotypical - I cannot say for sure as I have never tried being neurotypical. However, I can tell you exactly why it will not be a good idea with a child with ASD. These children already feel assaulted by the food they do not want to eat. Whether it is the smell, the color(s), the shape, the taste, the texture… it feels like an assault on their senses. Attempting to force themselves to eat whatever it is can result in becoming physically ill. This can in turn cause psychological trauma. The child may develop general anxiety around food, which can in the worst cases turn into eating disorders.

If your child does become physically ill, do not interpret this as an attempt to manipulate you. Obviously, I cannot rule it out as a possibility for every single child, but for the most part the child will be so overwhelmed by the attack on their senses that there is simply no room left to consider social consequences, much less actively manipulate others - and this ability in itself is rare in children with ASD.

Being unable to explain why you do not want to do something is frustrating on its own. We know that something is uncomfortable, but perhaps do not entirely know why or how, just that it feels wrong. For a child or young person with ASD, this can be difficult to put into words. The solution we are able to come up with is sometimes just as frustrating to those around us. We may simply say "no" over and over when told to eat, or become unresponsive. Those who are capable of crude manipulation may do anything to get themselves excused from the table.

If the problem is texture only, the solution is to find the textures that are appealing to the child, and do whatever you can to provide healthy options that have this texture. For example, your child may not like the crunchy feeling of chewing vegetables and/or biscuits. Biscuits can be avoided, but vegetables can be manipulated to have many different textures. They can be boiled, shredded, blended, juiced and whatever else you can think of. Try different things until you find a texture that your child can deal with.

The offending textures may change over time, which also means that previously offending textures may become non-offending at some point, but I may take years and there is no guarantee.

If the problem is only smell, color or taste, simply try to avoid the offending item(s) when possible, especially while the child is too young to be taught coping strategies effectively. Consult a professional about when your child is emotionally and cognitively mature enough to do this.

Slow Eating
One thing that can be frustrating for parents is that a child with ASD can very often be a slow eater. This is perhaps slightly less frustrating if you know why, even if you cannot change it. So here are some reasons why someone with ASD might be eating slowly.

Sensory environment
The issue here is that brain power is used on processing other things than food. Our brains pick up details at odd times, and this is difficult to control. Usually, it gets easier with age, but as a child you have no filter. So the light changing, for example, if it is sunny and then a cloud blocks the sunlight, the dampening of natural light that occurs is something we notice and focus on. Where your brain has learnt to note such details and then ignore them, many of us have to "manually" do this, and so it takes longer.

The list of things that can distract us from the act of eating is so numerous I will not even begin to try to list it. Suffice to say, any sensory input that changes is distracting.

Social environment/Manners
Another issue that can cause the process of eating to be slower is if the

mind is occupied with doing certain things right, or not doing certain things.

For example, some people on the spectrum love to talk, and once we get started we cannot stop. If your child is talkative, there can be some difficulty in balancing talking and eating, especially when one considers the rule: "Do not talk with food in your mouth." This is quite a problem if we are really excited about the conversation because then we constantly have to remind ourselves; "No, I am supposed to eat now."

Another issue that arises in this category is eating neatly. If you, as many of us do, have issues with fine motor skills, eating neatly – or just not getting food absolutely everywhere – can be problematic. Thus, our minds can become so occupied by holding knife and fork right, using them in such a manner that we do not make a mess, that there is not much left for actually eating, or simply that each movement becomes slow and deliberate, thereby slowing the dining process. Eating neatly is quite difficult for any child, but for a child with fine motor skill problems, or general problems with the proprioceptive sense, it is extra difficult.

You are asking this child to eat in such a way that they are not overly visible, audible, and when they have finished, their plate – and surroundings – should have no traces of eating ever having taken place; as if they were a ninja, completing a task without anyone noticing their presence.

Considering your child and their specific profile, and their age, think about what the current priority should be – is there something else they should be learning right now, rather than "ninja-eating"?

Analyzing food

A side effect to having sensory sensitivities and the detail focus that we do, is analyzing pretty much everything. This includes food. We notice temperature, texture, color, flavor and patterns. If a piece of meat has fat and cartilage, this will be the sort of thing we have to stop and deal with before we can eat the meat, because of the conflicting textures. Fat can taste very different to the meat it is attached to, and cartilage can be almost impossible to chew. So such things, while they may not bother you, are items on our list.

Next is planning how to eat the meal. One flavor affects the flavor of the next thing you eat (this may also explain why people with ASD, especially in their childhood, will finish eating one type of food before continuing to the next) combined, of course, with the problem that if you mix food-items on your fork, then it is not only the flavors that affect each other, but also textures mixing, which then creates a possibly disliked sensory experience.

In short, eating can take a lot of thought.

Eating Disorders

Whole books are written about eating disorders and both the reasons they develop but also how to treat them. I do not intend to cover this area, but merely give a short introduction to it. If your child has or is developing an eating disorder, you have to seek specialized help. There are people who work specifically with people who have both ASD and an eating disorder because people with ASD have a tendency not to respond to traditional treatment methods as expected. Therefore, in treatment of the eating disorder, ASD must also be taken into account. Statistically, the individuals with ASD most likely to develop eating disorders are girls around the age of 12-14. This does not mean they are the only ones who do, however, so please do not disregard any danger signs just because your child is not in this group.

The basis of an eating disorder can come from several sources, and I will quickly outline three. And please keep in mind that it needs not be one or the other, it can easily be a mixture of these. They may seem similar, but just like ASD, eating disorders are not as simple as once thought, which again, is why I recommend specialists if help is needed.

Inward-reacting

The inward-reacting profile can lead to depression from an early age. It can also lead to eating disorders. The thinking can go: "I am inherently wrong the way I am, but if I change, I can be okay." Changing, in this connection, can often be about losing weight, but there is also a variant which focuses on building muscle – looking more masculine or athletic. This is most common in boys. The goal is looking a certain way, and the outcome hoped for, will be either feeling better just because you look "better", or feeling better because others will like you more. It is not so much – at first – a need for control, but the idea that looking a certain way will fix things. One aspect of this is also that a lot of people with ASD have a really good memory, especially for bad experiences. Louise, a woman with Asperger's who has battled an eating disorder for many years, wrote to me in an email:

"I wasn't called fat more often than so many others. I just remember it. Every single time."

"We are bombarded with images and ideas from the media that speaks a clear language: People with success, people who are capable are slim. How many overweight singers are there? How many actors? In our world skinny equals success and fat equals failure. And to people to perceive things in a literal way and a very black and white way, there is no middle ground." (Louise Egelund Jensen, personal communication.)

There can be a desire to not just be thin, but to disappear. This is not necessarily related to suicidal thoughts, but is more about low self-worth. It is about wanting to be invisible to others. If they cannot see you, maybe they will leave you alone. People cannot make demands you feel you cannot live up to if you are invisible.

Control

The issue of control stems more often from anxiety than from depression. It is still an inward-reacting pattern in a sense, but the thinking is very different. This is less about how you look, and more about getting some measure of control of things. Control is the key word.

The thinking can be: "I cannot control anything else in my life, but I can control what I eat." This, then, becomes such a huge focus that controlling, for example, calorie intake and exercise schedules may become a special interest in itself. Having control of something, and keeping this control, can also be addictive if you feel anxious.

The control may also stem from something deeper and concrete, like being afraid of physical changes and trying to control how you look; trying to remain androgynous, keeping a child-like appearance. In this case, the eating disorder will begin at roughly the same time as puberty, and is rooted in the fear of change, which then turns into obsessive control of calories, weight, BMI... numbers. Keeping the change under control.

Another aspect of control is using control of food intake as a reward/punishment system for yourself. Not being 'good enough' in some way can be corrected with eating less.

Copying behavior

This one is a little convoluted. Girls on the spectrum have a higher tendency to mimic behavior, to copy others. This enables them to "fly under the radar" in terms of diagnosis because their outward behavior can seem "normal" if you do not know what to look for.

However, this tendency to mimic behavior can take over. The popular, skinny girl from school can become a focus to the extent that "I want to be like her" or even "I want to be her". Girls without ASD have those same thoughts, but they rarely take hold long term. Yet for girls on the spectrum (and more rarely, boys), it can become a special interest. It comes from a need to blend in in a positive way. It is not a desire to disappear in the crowd, but to fit into a group. The "skinny-ideal" that society has can become a rule for "how to be popular", and so become a part of the recipe or plan for how to become the person he/she has in their minds to be.

Once an eating disorder goes on for long enough, it will easily feel like a separate entity with which you have a relationship. You may know it is harming you, but it feels like it is the only thing you have. You can be afraid of letting go of it because you may return to what you were before: weak, alone, fat or whatever else was the triggering factor in your mind. This is one of the things that make eating disorders so difficult to treat.

Louise wrote to me that: *"The diagnosis [Asperger's Syndrome] opened the door to knowledge, a different and healthier knowledge of how I could create order in chaos, structure my life so I could deal with it again."*

Social Aspect

You can imagine, perhaps, that having to process the colors, textures, tastes and smells of each item of food, the brain can be quite busy when confronted with food. But there is an added problem in many households at dinnertime, which is the issue of eating together.

Rather than being able to focus solely on the sensory problem the food presents, we are now distracted by people talking, their facial expressions, voice intonations, gestures and emotions. It could be parents correcting siblings or ourselves on how we sit, handle the cutlery or merely a calm conversation. This means that the amount of information we have to process can exceed our capabilities, depending on the day's events, our age etc. The results can be a loss of appetite and if pushed, potentially a meltdown. Of course, no one wants this to happen, so the idea of any coping mechanism is not to have a young child appear normal, but first and foremost to make sure they are receiving nourishment.

Teaching us to sit up straight, eat neatly and socialize during a meal can take place later in childhood or in the teenage years, depending on the individual, but should not be your main priority in the younger years.

There are things that can make the social aspect of eating together less of a strain. Many people – not just on the spectrum – have an easier time conversing about difficult topics while walking or driving. Being beside a person rather than being face to face can lessen the emotional stress. For us, it is this way all the time. If we are not confronted with facial expressions, this means there is less information to process. Even as an adult, I prefer to eat in front of the television. This has nothing to do with the television itself – however entertaining the program might be – but rather that it allows me to keep the social aspect slightly dampened by having people beside me rather than in front of me. I do this especially after a stressful day, in order to not stress myself any further.

Your child might do something similar, even without knowing why they do it, and I would advise that you take their stress levels into account before discouraging this. It can be a good idea to have eating together be an optional thing, possibly in the form of the child opting out when he or she feels that they will be overwhelmed.

Depending on the age, this can be arranged in different appropriate ways. The key for the child is not to mix the sensory and social difficulties – so if you arrange it in such a way that you can see him or her, be sure that you are not asking them questions from across the room. "Are you alright?" "How is the food?" and "How was your day at school?" are not appropriate questions to ask during dinnertime. Generally speaking, you want to keep conversation directed at the child to a minimum during this time.

Again, every child on the spectrum is different, so take your child's profile into account.

Lunch at School

Lunchtime at school can be the most stressful environment the child encounters in day to day life. Not only do we have the sensory sensitivities from food, and the processing of social cues, but our senses are also challenged from the sound and light in the school environment. Fluorescent lighting is an issue for many people on the spectrum and in the most serious cases it is perceived as a neurotypical might perceive strobe lights. I do not think I need to point out that having to concentrate on anything will be difficult under such sensory circumstances. Furthermore, the sound atmosphere in most schools and especially in the school cafeteria can be compared to being in an echo valley or a cathedral with everyone talking at once. Even for many neurotypical people, this is unpleasant. Many of us have the problem that we pick up the sound from all the conversations, and our brains automatically try to decode all of this sound equally. So keeping up with one conversation over another in such an environment is very difficult, and causes misunderstandings and social and sensory stress. This, again, causes a loss in appetite, general anxiety, and meltdowns.

If at all possible, arrange for your child to eat in a smaller social environment, in a smaller room and with non-fluorescent light. This is very important because a child who does not eat during a school day will have to suffer through not only hunger, but also low blood sugar and exhaustion from lack of nourishment. In short, not a good foundation for learning.

Speaking to a young aspie about this topic, she told me;

"When I don't feel well, I have a lump in my stomach, and then I can't eat anything even though I want to. I try to eat, but after a few mouthfuls it becomes impossible."

PUBLIC PLACES

It is quite impossible to stay out of the public space with the way society works today. At some point you have to deal with the world. Public places present two big, unique challenges: the amount of social and sensory chaos, and the judgements made by strangers. The latter of the two does not really have a solution, and all you can do is learn to accept that people judge, and learn not to let their opinions ruin your day.

But there are coping mechanisms to apply to help deal with the sensory aspects.

The sensory experience

As with almost everything else concerning ASD, one of the elements to consider is the sensory one. The stress created by sound from many sources at once makes it difficult to be in an area with lots of people. Because people talk. A lot.

For you, this sound probably for the most part becomes background noise. But for us, it is a buzzing in our heads that distorts other sounds and makes it difficult to focus on what you are saying, or what we are supposed to be doing. Likewise, the many different and sometimes very sudden noises from machines, vehicles and such, means that merely on the auditory side, we can become overloaded very quickly. Of course, different people experience it differently, but this seems, from my experience, to be somewhat generally applicable. Suffice to say, it is uncomfortable.

Moving on to sight, there are colors and patterns we do not expect, and many different ones at the same time. This is frustrating and while this is all background for you, it is assaulting our senses, making it difficult to focus on the things we know we are expected to focus on, and the things we, ourselves, would rather be focusing on.

To cope with the sensory experience of being out in public, many aspies have developed ways of either blocking certain sensory inputs or decreasing the intensity of them. Those with sensitivity to light and/or eye contact may wear sunglasses. There are special colors of sunglasses that can be bought or custom made if the light sensitivity has to do with a specific range of light. When it comes to decreasing the intensity of eye contact, the sunglasses (especially the very dark ones) can feel like a protective barrier between you and everyone else. This is not an option for everyone but it does work for many. The colored lenses from the brand Irlen are a very popular choice amongst people with ASD.

As for the overwhelming amount of sound, many have taken to the options of either noise-reducing headphones and/or playing music whenever in public. Ellen describes doing this to reduce anxiety as well as dealing with sensory sensitivities in public places.

"I generally dislike being in public. I live in a big city, and with the noises being insane, I try to listen to music while I am out. It may sound weird to fight noise with more noise, but it works for me. It gives me something to concentrate on, If not, I get too caught up in everything that is going on. Strangers make me very uncomfortable. I freak out over what people might think of me and I know it's completely irrational, but I still do it." (Ellen, personal communication.)

Basic anxiety reaction

This does not apply to all, but some people with ASD, especially those who have experienced group bullying, may experience general anxiety from being in large crowds. It is not a phobia as such, but more a programmed anxiety that comes from expecting to get hurt. You do not know where the next jab is going to come from, but it might come and you are waiting for it.

A child or even adult might not realize where this feeling of anxiety comes from or why they are reacting that way, and because it is based on general anxiety, which does not necessarily present any outward symptoms – and it is not an anxiety attack – it will not be obvious to bystanders that the anxiety is even there.

This is especially important in cases of large crowds where the ability to move freely is hindered – as is can be in crowded school halls, for example, so it is best to try to avoid those sorts of situations if possible, also due to the resulting stress.

Expectation to be sociable

There is also an expectation to be social in public. Not to engage in deep conversation or an exploration of the identity of others or ourselves, however. The social expectations of the public sphere are the small things. Do I look this person in the eye or not? How will they react? Do not bump into people and try to avoid them bumping into you. Most importantly, do not stand out. When someone does bump into you, do not react. Just keep walking. If it is your fault, remember to apologize quickly, but do not expect others to. Be ready to respond in a polite way if someone engages you in small talk, but do not engage anyone yourself (on the off chance you actually wanted to) because you may misjudge your choice of conversationalist or not do it correctly, and they will be offended. This goes on and on, with these small odd ways of social interaction that are expected yet unwanted by us and neurotypicals alike (mostly in big cities), but nonetheless engaged in.

This is all annoying in different ways, depending on your age. When you are a very young child, you have no coping mechanisms to deal with the sensory sensitivities you have. This means there is no additional energy or attention to deal with the social bits. So when an elderly lady decides to ask you something or tell you something, it causes a meltdown rather than the cute smile she anticipated.

People stare at you when you read in public (perhaps just to see which book it is), or make comments about how rude it is to wear hoods or headphones inside. You, as parents, might very well be the target of comments about why your child is only wearing black clothes and never smiles – yet we hear it, too, we just cannot cope and do not know how to react.

As a teen, new problems begin as your peers begin to show one of two reactions to you. Either, it goes in the "positive" way, and they begin making sexual comments and flirting with you. This is highly uncomfortable because for the most part, our emotional maturity is delayed such that at the time our peers begin doing this, we are not thinking in remotely the same direction. It is also uncomfortable because we simply do not understand what is going on and also often because the way neurotypicals flirt at this age is not amusing or attractive to many of us. And yes, this happens in public, too. It also happens in school. As does the opposite and negative reaction. They will make comments about looks, fashion, lack of experience, nerdiness etc. They make fun of you, torment, and ridicule, and again, we do not know what to do about this. We do not know how to react in the situation, and we do not know where to direct our emotional reaction to it once it is over. Having to consciously think all things social through, means the proper response is delayed, which can cause its own set of problems.

For the most part, the problem with public places is the combination of sensory sensitivities and the pure presence of so many people being in our personal sphere, bumping into us, sometimes making rude comments or staring.

The conclusion must therefore be that if you intend to take us to the Natural History Museum, do not do it on a Saturday. If we must go on a weekend, try making sure we are the first ones in, for example, so the trip will be as quiet as possible. Do not do it when the tourists are out and about. As long as we are still learning how it all works, processing new areas and buildings and learning the rules of public conduct, it is best not to simultaneously push the limits in regard to crowds.

Amusement parks

These places have added layers to the sensory experience that most other places do not. The sounds we encounter of exited screams, many different pieces of music being played simultaneously, smells of different foods and people shoving things in your face, create a combination that is to many of us less exciting than it would be for neurotypical peers. To some children on the spectrum, this is rather a description of pure hell.

When investigating whether or not this is fun for your child, find a smaller amusement park and go there on a weekday if at all possible. This is the same strategy as with museums, shopping trips etc. Start small and push slowly. If your child likes these things, they will express this in one way or another, and if they hate it, you will know this, too.

Grocery stores and food courts

Here the issues concerning public places and food related sensory sensitivities combine. Even though the food is not right in front of us, we can still see it and smell it. In food courts there is an added problem in the pure number of people either using cutlery, messing with plastic and paper wrapping, chewing, talking, moving chairs and generally making lots of noise.

Generally, the strategy should be to get in and out of such places in a fair hurry, but without stressing your child. This means giving them information about what is going to happen, and an estimate on how quickly it will be over. "We are going to buy these items, and if I suddenly remember something else, I will try my best to be quick about it. I expect it will take about half an hour."

(This advice will not suffice for a child with severe autism, so if your child cannot cope with instructions like these, apply whichever version works for your child. Remember that this book concerns itself with the "Asperger's"-range of autism.)

Some children like these environments, especially stores. There can be a fascination with the combination of colors on a certain aisle, or with memorizing prices of certain things. Your child might even enjoy trying to add up how much the total will be, by memory, as you are picking up items.

If this is the case, allow them time to do this when possible, and in cases like adding up the total, help your child by making sure they have seen each item you put in the cart, and how many there are of them. If they get the correct total, they are obviously happy, yet if they are wrong, they might feel very badly. Encourage them to get it right, and help them to view mistakes as something positive that one can learn from.

Transportation

A lot of people on the spectrum have trouble with using public transportation. Some because they find it to be a confusing mess, some because you can never be able to predict with confidence if there are delays, if you can get the seat you feel comfortable in, how close you will have to stand to others and so on, and for yet others it is a matter of the sensory experiences and the fact that you know with almost complete certainty that it will be uncomfortable. Someone will either smell really badly, wear so much perfume that you feel you are choking or someone might stare at you.

There are so many possible uncomfortable things about it. On top of this, if you have to remember schedules, or you have a change that is difficult to make in time – possibly due to delays – or if you have a lot of changes to make, it can actually take up a lot of energy just to get where you are going.

I am lucky to live in a city where many things are reasonably close and our public transportation system can get you almost anywhere, but if I have to change more than twice, it gets to the point where even the idea of going on the trip is so stressful that I can have a hard time coping, and much more so if I am in a period of more depression or anxiety than normal.

If your child becomes stressed or anxious about using public transportation, see if it is possible that your child is driven instead and if it is not far, taxis could perhaps be considered.

Even though it might seem a luxury, the reduction in stress can be quite significant. Instead of trying to predict changes in sensory environment, social environment and recalling schedules for different modes of transportation, your child can then have time off, sitting in one means of transportation, and therefore arriving at their destination with much more energy than otherwise.

Specific modes of transportation are also common special interests. Trains and airplanes are most common, in my experience. If your child has a special interest in, for example, trains, they may very much enjoy taking the train and will speak endlessly to both you and strangers about what type of train you are travelling with, and details regarding its functionality and history. They may also want to take long trips that are unnecessary for your daily life, simply for the joy of being on the train. You may find that once they take public trains by themselves, they will want to go far and wide without remembering to tell you, precisely because they are so excited. For this reason, it may be a good idea to indulge this interest and to plan trips they want to take, so that you may be there to supervise them and make sure they get home safely.

CLOTHES, SHOES AND SHOPPING

Before you read this chapter, if you have not read the "Briefly About" sensory sensitivities and the chapter about public places, please do so now. Everything from them, applies here, too.

The sensory part of clothing

Clothes are tricky because the sensory sensitivities experienced by each individual on the spectrum are unique, at least to some extent. I can therefore not say that you should avoid certain types of clothes or shoes without knowing your child. Moreover, sensory sensitivities can change throughout a person's life, and so the fabrics or sensations that were unbearable as a child can perhaps become manageable later in life. I will try to give an idea of the general tendencies in sensory sensitivities with regard to clothing. Please keep in mind that your child may differ in their profile.

Generally speaking, children with proprioceptive difficulties tend to like tight-fitting clothes with long sleeves and long legs because this helps them know where their legs and arms end and where they are. These same children will be likely to respond well to weighted blankets/duvets (more about these in the last chapter).

Children with no proprioceptive difficulties tend to want less restrictive clothing, and may prefer anything loose fitting, even to the point of looking rather odd. At one point I preferred my boyfriend's hoodie, which was several sizes too big and looked like a very unbecoming dress on me. I did not care, and neither will your child.

In one area, almost every person with ASD is similar – comfort comes first. It is okay to look nice, of course, even fashionable. We do not mind looking good, but if it is not comfortable to wear, then we, as a rule, will not wear it.

You will be looking out for hard or scratchy fabrics, pants that are very tight-fitting in the waist (restricting movement and ability to sit comfortably), seams in odd places or that are pressing on the skin. Washing instruction labels can be either cut out or clothing with printed instructions selected instead.

I asked Katinka, a young girl with Asperger's syndrome, what she likes or dislikes about certain types of clothing:

"Wool is really scratchy, and is very uncomfortable to wear. When it comes to patterns, I really like dots and stripes are okay too, but checkered patterns take a lot of me to look at. It is overwhelming." (Katinka, personal communication.)

Your child will probably prefer certain colors and/or patterns, or as is the case with many, as few colors and patterns as possible. One adult with Asperger's expressed it as "reducing the sensory noise from my clothing". This means mostly black and white clothing, very dark blue is also often a favorite, no bold or obvious patterns (or even none at all), and no "frilly bits" for the girls.

Again, with age, some things can change, but this is the general rule, so it should give you an idea of what to do. Now, as for actual shopping.

Shopping for clothes

Stores are confusing places, and there are lots of people. But shopping for clothes and shoes adds an element that just is not much fun at all. Trying items on, dressing and undressing in a setting where you can hear people around you while in a dressing room. So you are dealing with the stress of noises and your parent waiting to see each item on, to judge if it fits etc. On top of that, the tags that are still on the clothing can be very distracting. Even if you might otherwise like wearing the item, the tag can be so uncomfortable that it is almost impossible to tell how you feel about the fabric. As a young child, before you have coping mechanisms to deal with uncomfortable sensory input, it is very difficult to bear for even a few seconds. Add to this the magnetic alarms attached to clothing in some stores – these can change the entirety of how an item feels to wear, either due to weight (pulling down in one side) or pressure (if it is tight-fitting clothing). This is difficult to deal with as a child but may become easier with age, when you get used to it.

Shoes are perhaps even more difficult. Because of the comfort of sameness, we like to wear the same pair of shoes until they are so worn that our toes stick out. But even if you then go and find a pair of shoes that are identical in shape, they will not have been broken in, and will therefore feel different. So almost any new pair of shoes are going to feel 'wrong' to us, rather than being exciting due to being shiny and new.

My advice is to let go a bit when it comes to insistence on sameness in clothing and shoes. Do not try to pack the wardrobe with colors and accessories. It will only confuse and if the child has any say, might very well never be worn. Go with what they like – and rather than buying the same shirt in five different colors, buy five identical shirts. That way, your child has a clean shirt on, but without the stress of it feeling different and weird compared to yesterday. If this causes trouble at school, teach your child to respond with "No, it is a different shirt than yesterday, but I just like to wear shirts that look the same."

The same goes for all other items of clothing – pants, underwear, socks. Buy identical ones instead of trying to make it fun.

Some girls with ASD will refuse to wear dresses, and others will not wear anything else, even if it is far too cold. Again, go with whatever is comfortable for them, and just try to adapt to the weather and climate in some way. Solutions can always be found, sometimes, it just takes a lot of trial and error.

However, as Jimmi, a man with Asperger's wrote to me:

"For many people with ASD, buying clothes and shoes is something we want over with. We generally don't care about fashion, although there are always exceptions to the rule. I do think it can be beneficial for young people with ASD to buy clothes and shoes that are either "in" right now, or have a more classic style, simply to avoid attention and bullying due to one's clothes. Of course, this does not mean you will not be bullied for other things. It can be good to have help for clothes- and shoe-shopping [from an adult], if you don't have a good friend who wants to go shopping with you." (Jimmi, personal communication.)

Suddenly wanting something new

This happens for us, too. Suddenly, some day, a whim strikes us that we want pink socks instead of black ones. The truth is, very often we did not think it through. Like any other child, we do not know ourselves well enough to realize that even though it is fun today, by lunch tomorrow at school, we will want our black socks back on.

Encourage these whims, but make sure there is a back-up plan. That is, put the black socks into the school bag and tell your child "I am putting your black socks in this pocket of your bag. If you want to switch socks at some point, you can do so." That way, when the thought hits that 'Oh! My socks are pink, I don't want pink socks on anymore!' it does not reach the meltdown stage as easily, because you have already provided the solution.

VACATIONS

Everyone loves a good vacation. Taking some time off, seeing new places. Everyone that is, except the unprepared autistic person. First of all, please make sure you have read the chapters on public places and food because that content also applies here.

Do research and find pictures
Going to a new place can be really exciting and interesting and some people like not knowing what to expect. This cannot be said for people with ASD. We like to know. We like to be prepared. How prepared we want to be depends on the individual, but some degree of knowing what we are getting into is always nice.

So to satisfy this, and avoid any anxiety that might otherwise arise, you should prepare yourself to talk a lot about where you are going and what you will be doing there.

The first thing is to do some research about the place you are going. Ask your child to go online and find information and pictures, in order to engage them in the process and planning. Find out which places you and your child want to see, sights and museums or whatever it might be. The more you can involve the child in doing this research, the more prepared they will be for the trip.

Keep some structure
When some people go on vacation they prefer to change their daily routines around and adopt a more casual view of things. Depending on your child and their profile, they can either deal with this or they cannot. The younger the child is, the less likely it is that they can, so I suggest keeping some of the daily structure even though all is not possible. Try to keep the morning routine as closely to normal as possible, giving your child the most positive and predictable beginning to their day possible. This will hopefully reduce stress and anxiety. Keep in mind that some children with ASD would prefer that no changes ever occur. These children can be upset at not having to go to school – even if they are unhappy there. If your child needs a higher level of structure to their day, it is essential to keep this, even when on vacation. As Rebecca told me;

"Though I'm not a big fan of going to school anymore, I don't like having vacations. Things get changed and daily life becomes unstructured. If I go on holiday somewhere, the days have to be planned carefully. If there are breaks in the day, it should be when I am tired, for example after having been out for a long time." (Rebecca, personal communication.)

61

Plan for different situations

Make sure there are plans that take different things into account, for example, if it rains one day, we will do this instead. We are planning to sleep in on this day, but if we wake up early anyway, we can do this. In general, planning and schedules are great – visual ones are best.

Make a plan for the day you are leaving. What are you going to do to get to the airport if you are going on a plane? What time does check-in start? Make sure you have time to walk around the airport – and even more if your child is interested in planes and airports.

Again, the need for planning may very well decrease with age and familiarity, and spontaneity can be introduced by the child.

Take their profile into account – how much planning do they want/need, how many times do they need to go through the plans etc. This all differs for each individual. I recommend erring on the side of overdoing it and being slightly annoying, rather than underestimating how anxious your child will get, at least the first time you go traveling. Once you have a better idea of how your child reacts in this type of situation, it will be easier to know what to do next time.

New sensory experiences

Depending on how far away you are going, more and more sensory experiences will change. The smells, colors, climate, and intensity of sunlight can all change dramatically. This means that your child will be adjusting to a whole new set of sensory inputs and experiences, and possible previously undiscovered sensitivities may now be 'triggered' by stress and anxiety.

Some changes can be very positive, and some are unexpected, counterintuitive, or do not make sense, for example, I may have to wear sunglasses during both summer and winter in Europe, but not always on other continents – the sunlight hurts my eyes less, as it is softer somehow.

If your child is used to feeling uncomfortably hot or cold, going somewhere with a colder or warmer climate respectively, can also provide a sensory break in that regard and bring more energy or lessen stress.

Both personal experience and conversations with others on the spectrum indicate that we generally need a few days to adjust to a new place and to recover from travel. I always make sure that the first few days of a vacation are reserved for relaxing and calmly exploring the nearby area of the hotel. I also make sure that I have a few days off when I come home in order to readjust to everyday life. Both of these are crucial to coping with travel for me, and many others express the same need for time to adjust and readjust.

New social cultures and rules

Other countries also have other social cultures and rules to follow. It is best to be prepared for these, so include them in your research. Certain hand gestures might mean other things than they do in your culture – a thumbs up can be rude, for example, or burping while eating can be considered the polite thing to do.

While such things can be confusing, they can also be fun and exciting, and present a chance to teach your child about how social norms can differ across the globe. It is a very good chance to expose your child to the fact that even people without ASD can make social mistakes if they do not know the rules, but that one can learn the rules and apply them, which results in fewer misunderstandings.

Special interests in foreign cultures

Children with ASD develop special interests in all sorts of things, and one rather common interest is a different culture – usually one very different from one's own and sometimes one that no longer exists. It can be ancient Rome, Egypt or China, or it can be modern Japan. It can be almost anything. But in any case, such a special interest often develops into a great enthusiasm to travel to places that have to do with it, and can provide the courage to go places and do things they normally would be afraid to do. It can stave off stress, exhaustion and anxiety to a great degree – as we become so immersed in the interest and exploring it that it takes priority. The stress and/or exhaustion will catch up at some point, but you may be surprised at how long it takes.

Let your child explore, but try to protect them a bit. They can become so immersed that they do not feel hunger or thirst, and it will be your problem to get them to sit down and eat. Of course, one great thing here is that you can test some things out concerning food, as traditional dishes from the culture of interest will perhaps have some draw.

MY ROOM

As a child, even as early as age 6 or 7, my room was my favorite place in the world. I did not have a lock on the door yet, but I would have a hook on the door before I turned 10. Knowing that it was my room and no one could come in unless I wanted it, was my greatest relief.

My room was almost always incredibly messy. Not dirty, per se, just messy. There were Lego and dinosaur toys all over the floor. I wanted it that way. I liked it.

I spent most of my time in there, and I was never unhappy there. In my room, with my toys, I could enter a different world that no one could touch. No one could take it away. As soon as I got my first stereo, the toys were replaced and music now allowed me a new and different fictional and emotional world to enter. I never wanted to leave. I still do not.

Any parent of a normal child would have probably been concerned. When a child of 10 has only one or two friends and spends as much time as they are allowed to in solitude in their room, most parents get concerned.

But I think my mother realized that solitude was more preferable to me than being forced to socialize. She realized that my room was my sanctuary. My haven.

Solitude is so very valuable to people on the spectrum. We need it like we need food and sleep. It provides the emotional and mental restorative, the peace, which allows us to continue facing the world. Think of it as meditation. Time spent in solitude, engaged in a special interest is great, but, it is also the knowledge that you will not be interrupted that makes the difference.

Understanding the language and rules

My room. It is a room that is mine. Property. Territory. Mine. This is important because of the way we understand language vs the way others/you do. When you say "Your room" to a child, you probably mean "Your room is in my house, which means there are certain rules that apply that you do not get to control, because I am still the boss. We call it your room because that is what people call it, but it is actually ultimately under my control because it is part of my house, or to paraphrase; "It is my house and you are given use of that room for as long as you live here."

We can compare it to governments and plots of land within them. You buy land, and that makes it yours, but it still ultimately belongs to the country it is in, and if you break the laws of the country – whether you do it on your land or not – you are in trouble. Likewise, if I do not follow my parents' rules that apply to my room, I am in trouble. People on the spectrum do not understand this. It is my room. If it is not mine, do not call it mine. And if you want to make agreements about which laws apply in my room, they had better be reasonable, and you have to provide the reason along with the rule/law.

You will have an even worse time having a child with ASD in your house if they do not have a room to call theirs, because we need to have a place we can go and know that we are alone and will not be disturbed.

So this is all about making sensible rules for that room.

"You have to clean your room so it does not get too dirty, because otherwise little bugs start taking over and they will get into the rest of the house/apartment even though I clean it. I do not want these bugs because..."

"You have to tidy your room every week/day/whenever because this makes it easier and faster to clean. It also means you always know where your things are – they will not get lost. It means you will not be as overwhelmed by having to tidy because there will not be quite as much."

Your guests and my room

One rule most parents want to enforce is that the room has to be tidy when guests come over. This is not an easy rule to try to convince a person with ASD of, and here is why:

If they are your guests, they do not need to see and especially do not need to enter my room. I do not want them there. If they have kids, and those kids are given access to my room, they will want to play with my toys. I do not want them to. If I do want them to, it is no use tidying before anyway, because they will make a mess. In short – my room is not yours to show off to your friends, even if I like them, and it is my choice if I let people in there. It is my choice if others get to touch my stuff.

Unfortunately, I cannot recommend a way for you to get your way on this point because it is not logical. If you want it your way, try rewards. ASD-logic dictates you are wrong on this matter, and so you will have to make it worth their while to tidy and show their room to your guests. However, if your child feels very private about their room, it can feel like a violation to be 'forced' to show it to people they do not feel quite as comfortable with. When it comes to trust, like so much else, we tend to fall in extremes, and so your child may have an incredibly easy time trusting new people, but more likely, it will take them a long time to develop trust. It can be months or even years. So please take this into account when considering who you are asking your child to let into their safe haven.

Design and decor

Most parents will want a happy room for their child. One with happy items and colors, one that is bright and "gives energy". However, children with ASD have a very firm idea of how they want their room to be, regardless of what their parents might think.

One person I know had lots of pillows with different colors on each side because that way, she could turn them over to whichever pattern of colors was pleasing to her on that day, all depending on her mood. This might be something most parents would find fun or, at the very least, acceptable.

I always wanted my curtains closed because when they are open I feel exposed and anxious. I also wanted dark colors because they soothe me. This is not something all parents are likely to understand, and certainly not something I could explain at age ten. I just knew what I wanted.

I am naturally not suggesting you follow every whim your child has, and especially not if their requests change often. I can imagine how hard work it would be to paint their walls a new color every week. However, I am saying that although our tastes can be very unconventional and sometimes very precise in detail, there is usually a reason behind our wishes for how we want our rooms to look, and if you can find some way to accommodate our wishes, you might very well have fulfilled a deep emotional need, even though we do not have the words to tell you this.

What it means to me

As I mentioned, my room was always my favorite place to be. It is for many, if not most, children with ASD. It provides us with solitude and downtime. This is where we can breathe. It is the place where all expectations from other people, all the pressure we are constantly under, disappear. I am not sure if I can truly explain the peace and relief of being alone in your room.

Perhaps you can compare it to a primal human, alone, being chased by a predator of some kind – let's make it a lion – and finally, after a whole day of running and dodging attacks, this human finds a cave that the lion cannot enter. It is still outside, but at least it cannot come in.

This is the immensity of the relief that I, and so many others, feel when we come home from school and lock ourselves in our room. It is our safe haven, our stronghold. The only physical place where we feel truly free. Due to our strong attachment to this private space, there can also be a reluctance to let others come in and see it. As previously mentioned, it can almost feel like a violation because people get too close that way. A young woman with ASD wrote to me that:

"My room has always been a free space; a place I could be myself. That's why I have always been very worried of potential friends' reactions to my room, with it being so personal and private for me. Therefore, I also prefer meeting my friends at their place or other places, because then I have my private sphere at home, where I can unwind without any social demands." (Signe, personal communication.)

If our special interest can also be indulged in within the confines of our room that only makes the relief and peace greater. Unfortunately, this has a side effect, because it means that many of us do not actually ever want to come back out. For most, it gets easier with age and maturity to control the urge to stay in our cave, and actually go out and face responsibility, school, work and people. For others, it gets harder. Usually, due to bullying, anxiety, depression or simply a lack of confidence, which normally builds for years before we truly become hermits. However, this outcome is very rare for those who are diagnosed before adulthood and given the necessary support.

The key words there are "necessary support" as there can be quite a difference between the support we need, and the "treatments" imposed on us by people who want to cure us.

Lifelong necessity

Many parents may want to try all sorts of things to get their child out of their rooms and have hopes that we will become "more social" with age.

The fact is that I have never heard anyone on the spectrum say that they could live with another person without having a room to themselves. It can be an office, a gaming room or a workshop. Usually it has something to do with the special interest. But the room is there. It might be called something else, but it is a room that is only theirs, and which any partner does not simply enter without permission

So when your child is an adult and may want to move in with someone, they should make sure that the place they move to has enough room for "their room".

I experienced this problem myself when moving in with a boyfriend and having a shared office, thinking that as long as there was one more room aside from the bedroom and living room it would be fine, but realizing that, over a few months, I became much more tense and less social because the lack of a room and alone-time was stressing me. The solution of being home alone whenever he was out helped to some degree but it is far from optimal. The need for "my room" has not disappeared og diminished for any adult on the spectrum I have ever met. This, incidentally, does not diminish our love for the people around us, which is important to remember. It is equally as important to teach us to communicate this fact to future partners, because being social and meeting social expectations is exhausting for us no matter how much we love and adore the people we are social with, and the more our needs for a safe haven and alone-time are met, the more energy we will have to meet expectations and communicate in general.

How you can help

Your child's room should be their place where they are safe and happy. It should allow, if possible, for their special interest to be engaged in, which will go a great way towards happiness within that space.

If there has to be rules regarding the room, the time spent in it, when to come out etc., make sure these have sensible reasons and that you explain the reasons so the child understands why they are in place because children, with ASD are not likely to adhere to authority if said authority seems to them to be unreasonable and unfair.

It is my opinion that some rules should be in place. Things like bedtime before school nights, keeping a somewhat tidy and clean room (not 'Keeping Up Appearances'-clean, just so it is not unhealthy), coming out for dinner etc., are all good things. But the "why" is very important to a child (or an adult) with ASD so I would suggest it might be productive for parents without ASD to think about the "why" and communicate this clearly to the child.

Respect your child's door. If it is closed, you knock. It may seem a silly thing that a parent should knock before entering, but it serves several functions. First, it shows your child that you respect their privacy, which is incredibly important to them. Secondly, it gives them a moment to prepare that something social is about to occur, which again, is incredibly important to them.

So please knock and respect their response when this is sensible. Wait for them to say "come in" because, of course, your child should be instructed that saying "come in" is the polite way to respond when someone knocks. If there are siblings, make sure they know and understand this, and for peace in the house, it might be good to have similar practices with them. Make sure the room is never a punishment, as again, you want it to be a place of safety and happiness.

TOYS, GAMES AND PLAY

Kids love their toys and play games that are fun to them. There is nothing unusual about exploring the world through play. What may be very unusual about children with ASD is the things about the world they feel the need to explore, and how many times they explore the same thing.

But like any other child, we play to have fun and to learn. We play to understand the world and explore narratives. We may actually play more than other children do, because the things explored by other children through social contact, we may very well explore on our own instead. Do not worry about this. This is a part of our natural development.

Attachment to toys

People on the spectrum usually have a great emotional attachment to certain objects. They also have a strong sense of justice, of right and wrong. Sometimes their logic can be hard to follow for other people, but it makes sense to us.

The objects we are attached to depend on age, special interest and so forth. Almost every child has a favorite toy which is the best thing to play with and which they perhaps feel slightly territorial about. A child with ASD also has favorite toys, but like with their room, their sense of what belongs to them is slightly more defined than you might expect. So their reaction to another child playing with and perhaps breaking their toy, will be greater, and will last longer.

"I remember a birthday in my early childhood, I must have been six, maybe seven. It stands out in my mind as one of the first times I (or perhaps my parents) invited the children from my class to our house. Overall the party went well until I discovered that the other children had been playing with my Lego, which in itself wasn't bad; what upset me was that they had taken apart my meticulously assembled constructions. This was a breach of trust which I could not bear, and as a result this was the only birthday I celebrated with non-family members until well into my teens, although by that time, this event was no longer my reason for not having a party, rather it had just never become a tradition for me to celebrate birthdays or other occasions with other students from my class." (Michael, personal communication)

A neurotypical child might get angry or sad in that same situation but, in time, they will most likely want to have another party. A child with ASD is set in their decision not only because they can be stubborn, but also because the betrayal or hurt experienced when other children have broken a toy of theirs, is so great that it is not forgotten or forgiven easily. In other words, my favorite toy is more important to me than any number of

71

birthday parties. In this regard, it also matters that to us, a birthday party is not necessarily fun, especially if it includes, as it does in some cultures, forced socialization and play with classmates rather than only the children we consider to be friends.

The games we play

Our choice of games and play is different than that of our neurotypical peers, and our reaction to being made to play under the rules of others is also different. We may play with toys expected of our gender, but often not in the same manner. Girls, if they are interested in dolls at all, will often use dolls to recreate a social interaction from their day repeatedly, in an attempt to understand what happened, rather than making up their own stories. Boys may play with their Lego, but be much more focused on the details of what they are building and will often leave their creations standing. Building or setting something up can be the whole game for us, rather than "actually playing" with the toys, as Liane Holliday Willey talks about in her book "Pretending to be Normal":

"Like with my tea parties, the fun came from setting up and arranging things. Maybe this desire to organize things rather than play with things, is the reason I never had a great interest in my peers. They always wanted to use the things I had so carefully arranged. They would want to rearrange and redo. They did not let me control the environment. They did not act the way I thought they should act. Children needed more freedom than I could provide them" (Willey 1999, p.16-17).

Children with ASD seem perhaps to be less concerned with the gender identity associated with specific toys, and more occupied with how much fun they are to us, or what we might learn by playing with them.

Most importantly, the games tend not to involve others. If they are social in nature, we want to control all the characters involved. Letting another person control a character is a wildcard, as they may have other plans for the game which will then leave us confused and trying to catch up with the thought process of another, rather than enjoying the game.

I recall attempting to let a friend into one of my games and finding it, at times, perfectly fine. However, I also recall much greater joy playing the same game on my own, because there was less energy spent on trying to anticipate what my friend would do, and more on simply enjoying the game.

Social games will often be either exact or very close reenactments of observed events or something on television; either a story we love or a part of a story that contains something we do not quite understand. Reenacting it gives us the chance to either re-experience the joy of the story at will, or attempt to learn through repetition, whatever it is we do not understand.

We may also invent our own worlds, taking inspiration from other stories or building something from scratch. These worlds can be highly complicated and detailed, and we have no trouble remembering facts and details from this created world. I have heard concerns from parents that this world either takes over the child's whole life, social and otherwise, or that perhaps the child is not able to differentiate between make-believe and reality. In both cases, I would generally not worry. The reason it seems to take over our lives, is because it becomes a special interest like any other. The joy we experience there is so great that nothing can match it. I have yet to hear about a person with ASD who cannot tell a made-up world from reality, yet it may seem that way because we enjoy the other world so much that we may at times "check out" of reality and refuse to participate. This is likely to pass on its own, and otherwise we can, for the most part, be baited back into reality by someone asking us about the world we have created. Social interaction can be easily initiated in this way, and from there, it can evolve. Whether done by an adult or a child does not matter in this case. What does matter is that we are not ridiculed for the created world, but instead complimented on our creativity. Keep in mind that the world your child has created, may lead them to write the next "Harry Potter" or "Lord of the Rings".

Some children engage in writing their own fiction from a relatively early age, and again, this can be extensive and detailed and if a special interest includes, for example, the creation of a world or fascination with a character, we may be deeply intrigued with writing genealogies, descriptions, lists and drawing maps.

Again, these are solitary activities, but should not be discouraged for that reason. These are activities that bring us joy and help us to develop and increase skills that may be very useful in life.

In the playground, we tend to be on the periphery, observing rather than joining in. We may also actively hide from the other children, finding a quiet area. This may be due to bullying, but can just as easily be a matter of the playground being a stressful sensory environment for us.

Even board games are turned into solitary games, by playing all sides ourselves. In monopoly, we may choose to play as three players, actively trying to defeat each players' opponents. We do this to develop game strategies, but also to have a chance to experience the game without the social aspect and potential ridicule, should we lose. By playing all sides ourselves, we always win, and therefore do not have to feel defeated, which, of course, is more common amongst children who have been bullied or ridiculed in this context, but worth mentioning to avoid the confusion that a child displaying this behavior "wants someone to play with" or is "lonely". They are experiencing the game in a way that feels safe to them. Alone does not equate to lonely.

Computer games

With the increase in the amount of computer games available, and the age at which many children begin playing, I feel it important to include a section on this, specifically.

Many games are solitary and do not include social activity of any kind, however, this does not mean that your child cannot learn skills from playing. Many games require logic, to think quickly, to recognize patterns etc. All skills that many children with ASD are naturally good at. Such games should be encouraged, though possibly in some moderation, depending on the child's age.

It is also, in many cases, beneficial for an adult to engage in the game with the child, and help them understand the rules of the game, and keep their confidence up when training skills that the child is not good at. Compliment intelligence and creativity, and encourage a positive view of mistakes.

When the child reaches an age where games like World of Warcraft (WoW) can be played, I feel this game and others like it should be encouraged for one great reason in particular; This is the sort of game we can play while learning social skills and using them in real time.

A teenage or adult mentor can have their own account and play with the child, using the private chat functions (in WoW, this is called a whisper) to explain social rules when needed, as well as any game mechanics the child does not yet know. This type of game excludes the need to read voice intonation, facial expression and body language, so social interaction requires much less energy and can therefore be participated in for greater lengths of time, and without the consequence of social exhaustion at least to the same degree.

The problem can be some measure of addiction to the game, in part because the people we meet online can be our only perceived friends for long periods of time, and in part because we can become very good at it and be praised by online friends and acquaintances, and therefore, feel a sense of achievement and social acceptance which is so rare in the "real world".

As a parent, you must understand that the friends made online are real people, and if we have an appointment with them in the game, to meet for roleplaying or raiding or whatever it might be, the responsibility we feel to uphold the agreement is just as real as we would feel towards any other person. Obviously, feeling such responsibility is a good personality trait, and should therefore be encouraged, as it naturally would be if the appointment was to go to someone's house for a playdate. Obviously, it should also be encouraged that the child informs you of their appointments with online friends, especially if they influence, for example, when your child may need to leave the dinner table. What should not be encouraged is neglecting "real world" friends in favor of online ones. Keep in mind that "real world" friends can also be engaged with through this medium, and that it may be a good way to socialize, due in part to the text based conversation. Jimmi, a man with Asperger's gave me his opinion on this topic, saying:

"Some of the positives about playing computer games is that you can unwind and use it as downtime, that you can strengthen your ability to focus and get better at English [if you are not a native speaker]. For people with ASD it's also an easy way to be social, because you are doing something specific together. It can also be a good escape from reality, if you are pressured in real life." (Jimmi, personal communication.)

Depending on the child's age, keep in mind whether previous special interests have become more moderate in time, and regulate your own response to the amount of time played accordingly. It works best to show interest and find ways to turn the interest into something that takes place in the "real world". For example, when your child is old enough, you may suggest going with them to a gaming convention where they can meet people who also love these games.

Computer games do not have to be social, however. A young woman with ASD explained that she uses certain games to de-stress:

"The right computer game is a blessing. It gives a feeling of repetition, a puzzle which on a very stressful day can untangle the mental ball of yarn. World of Warcraft, Ookami and Assassins Creed are really good for this purpose, I think. Other computer games drain me of energy, and I can only play them on good days. These are more complicated games with a high pace, which I have to think about or that have storylines." (Signe, personal communication.)

How you can help

Accept that your child is not going to play the way other children do. Engage in conversation about the games and toys that have their interest. Do not force your involvement in the game, but make yourself available. By showing interest in your child's interest, you teach them to interact with others about it, and they may be more inclined to make their interest a part of their social life. You also show them that you are interested in what they are doing, which likely makes them very happy. It is vital that you show and say that your child's choice of toys, manner of play and whatever level of engagement with other children, is good, intelligent and creative, because of possible criticism your child may meet from other adults.

You, as a parent, cannot do much to counter the bullying of children, but you can counter the comments made by teachers and other professionals, as well as those made by family members who may feel the need to correct your child and their play.

Your child must know, without a doubt, that you are supportive of whether or not they want to play with certain children, that you trust their judgement in choice of play-partners, that you like their choice of toy and think their way of playing is no less valuable than that of other children. They must know this, so that when a teacher tells them how to play and who to play with, they know that they always have you on their side, while, of course, they still have to be polite and respectful to both the teacher and other children.

GUESTS

The assumption in this chapter is that the guests in question are yours. Playdates are covered in in the chapter about friends.

Inform your guests

This is rule no. 1. All guests that your child will be interacting with should be informed either of the diagnosis or of anything different they are likely to encounter. The latter is most important. They do not necessarily need to know "My child has Asperger's/Autism", but they do need to know "My child cannot participate in conversation while eating, because it is overwhelming". Do not turn it into a problem, and do not expose your child to the conversation you have with your guests – do it over the phone, or at least away from the child. Making a remark in front of him/her about a certain way that he/she is different can make him/her feel anxious. Not necessarily embarrassed, but probably just feeling pressure from attention being on them in a way that they do not know how to react to.

If something unexpected happens, try to take it in stride and communicate your way through the situation. As always, the most important rule is to stay calm. Do not panic if your guests say or do the wrong thing with your child, even if your child acts out. Breathe, calm down, and handle the situation like you would any other day. And of course, do not blame the child or the guests for things going wrong. Your child reacts as well as they are capable of, and your guests cannot be expected to remember everything about your child's profile. Even if they also have a child or family member with autism, their profile is likely different.

Manners and social expectations

Be aware that when you have guests over, you may have a subconsciously increased need for behavioral perfection. It can also be entirely conscious, of course, but this should be given up as it will not do any good. Since you will be more anxious this will make your child more anxious. You will have a greater risk of reacting negatively towards actions undertaken by your child, to which you might normally not react, and so forth. Neurotypical children may handle this okay but a child with ASD will not.

Instead, keep things as close to normal as you can because this will meet your child's need for sameness, and thereby you will avoid anxiety on their part. You should not expect your child to engage in small-talk because while children without ASD can feel uncomfortable and bored with talking to adults about school or friends, a child with ASD may feel downright frightened at the concept. Your child might, however, be thrilled to lecture about their special interest, and if they play a musical instrument or write stories, they may be keen on showing their skills to anyone who will listen, and sometimes also those who will not. But small-talk is not likely within their skillset.

Dining ritual changes

There are several aspects to this part of having guests. There are new people at the dining table and family members do not necessarily sit where they usually do, but if you can, make sure they do. And most importantly do not change where your child sits.

The fact alone that there are new people around the dining table can cause all sorts of confusion and tension in your child. This may further influence their eating habits. If it does, there is a reason, so try not to push them. Rather, if possible, have them sit alone to eat if this makes them more comfortable than being at the table. If nothing makes them comfortable, try to accommodate them and create positive experiences with the guests through appealing to their special interest or giving them access to pleasant sensory experiences. They may have a blanket of a particular fabric, a stress ball or if necessary, a music player with a headset. If possible, communicate to your guests beforehand if such things will be at the dining table in order to avoid confusion or them making comments while there.

Also, when there are guests for dinner, there is conversation between courses for the adults to engage in. For the child, it will often feel like a void and, normally, we would fill that void with something: either go and play until the next course is on the table or sit with the iPad or help in the kitchen, whatever your child normally does if there are two or more courses. Try to keep this ritual for them even if it may seem rude to your guests. Try to explain to them that your child has certain rituals that make them feel happy and safe, and that any change in their day-to-day life is very upsetting. You may tell them the specific diagnosis or not. What is important is that your guests know not to scold your child for these behaviors, even when you are visiting them, and if they can, not to mention it at all. The inactivity between courses is especially grueling if we know there is dessert and many kids like dessert, and most kids will bounce around asking when dessert will be served.

When you have a child on the spectrum, you have the perfect solution to this; when your child wants to know, simply give them a time-frame to work within. You can either say a certain time, or if your child deals well with the concept, say that it will be before a certain time, giving yourself ample room to not stress. For example, if dinner starts at 6pm, you can tell your child: "Dessert will be served before 9pm." The time frame should be one that your child can work with and should take their age and emotional maturity into account. Waiting is something we all have to learn.

Lastly, the earlier your child can be excused from the dinner table, the better. The exception is if your child is happily giving lectures about everything they know, of course. But, generally speaking, it is an uncomfortable situation for us, and more so the younger we are, and the sooner we can escape into our room and play or read or engage in an interest, the better. You can also put a time-frame on this, if your child responds well to this coping mechanism.

Familiarity with guests

Our stress and anxiety responses to guests can be vastly different, depending on whether or not we know the people in question. When we meet new people, we first have to figure a lot of things out about them. Unlike people who are not on the spectrum, we have a harder time generalizing our experiences from one "type" of person to another, similar "type" of person. On the other extreme, there can be a tendency to over-generalize.

When a neurotypical person meets, for example, a priest, they will use their former experiences and connotations with priests to form a quick idea of who they are dealing with. They might think of traits like god-fearing, good, helpful, calm, trustworthy, knowledgeable, a confidante and so on.

The picture they form in your mind of the concept "priest" is then evolved into the picture of "this priest", as they get to know him better. So while there is an element of prejudice, it is a useful form of it, in most cases.

We, on the spectrum, have a hard time associating traits with concepts, and transferring them to new people who fit said concepts. This means that, when we meet a new person, we start with a blank slate and have to fit in every trait as we go along. So it takes longer for us to trust people and feel comfortable around them. Once we know someone, there is much less anxiety associated with being around them because the slate has been filled in, and we know who we are dealing with.

So while you have to prepare us extensively to meet someone new, you can give shorter notice (though preferably still a few days) if we are meeting with people who are familiar to us.

When to have people over

When making plans for people to visit, consider how much energy your child has to cope with the extra social expectations and the knowledge that other people are in the house. This really goes for all guests and also for playdates. If your child is already worn out from the day at school, it might not be good to stress them further. If they have school or an event the day after, then social activity today may take away the energy they need for tomorrow.

When I speak to other aspies about guests, they mostly say one of two things. The slightly rarer statement will be that they really like having guests over, but that it is draining, so it has to be planned around in order to avoid being completely run down for several days after.

The more typical statement will be some version of this:

"Home is my sanctuary. It is where I relax, recharge and retreat after a day of people and the outside world. Therefore, I don't particularly enjoy guests. Even when I finally leave the draining dinner of questions and small talk, I still can't really relax. Other people at my house, even in another room, is not optimal for my much needed alone time." (Ellen, personal communication.)

This, of course, results in even more alone time being needed, than would otherwise have been the case.

Family holidays

Naturally, the advice about food also applies here. If there is a traditional dish associated with a particular holiday, for example, Easter or Christmas, that makes your child ill, either to eat or to even smell, please do not force the child to deal with it. Tough love is not an approach that will produce any desired results.

Give the child the option to go and be alone, whether you are at home or at a family member's house. This is a fantastic coping mechanism, as it provides an escape route. Most children will actually be able to cope with more social activity when they have the knowledge that they can leave at any time.

Be aware that your expectations of social activity may be higher. Your family members may also expect more of your child during these holidays. Try to decrease these, and if you feel that your family members are hurt by your child not participating more, tell them that your child is doing as well as they can.

One more issue that can arise for Christmas and birthdays, is giving and receiving gifts and having polite responses to getting unwanted items. Unfortunately, we all experience getting a gift that we did not really want, so try to discuss in advance and create Social Stories and roleplaying games about giving and receiving gifts, exploring the emotions felt by the parties involved, depending on the reaction they get from each other.

Also, simple rules-of-life can work really well; "If you do not say 'thank you', people will be hurt and think you are ungrateful, and they will not want to get you something next year."

You should be aware, however, that your child will then expect everyone to follow this rule, every time, and get annoyed and confused if they do not. If the rule applies to them, it applies to all.

FRIENDS

One of the most common concerns I hear from parents is that they feel their child has very few friends and therefore must be lonely. Most people with ASD do feel lonely, but it is not necessarily because they lack friends. It is because we have a very hard time finding people who truly understand us. So the best chance at not feeling lonely is to find another person with ASD who has similar traits and interests. That being said, most of us also like to have a few friends, no matter if they have ASD or not. For most, one really good friend is all we need. This is especially true in childhood.

For many, the number of friends they can cope with will slightly increase as they get older. One friend might take all one's energy as a child, two is plenty during the teenage years and so on.

Finding friends
We can have real trouble finding friends, both as children and throughout the rest of our lives. There can be several reasons but, mostly, it boils down to social awkwardness and naivety. We are unsure of how to initiate contact, how to maintain it and how to get positive attention from peers. Even when we get positive attention, we can be remarkably bad at spotting the signs of friendship from other children, as explained by Liane Holliday Willey:

"Looking far over my shoulder, I can call to mind people who must have been interested in friendship. I can see a boy I knew as if it was yesterday. I can remember his face and the expressions he made as we talked. Today if he looked at me like he did then, I believe I would have seen the kindness and gentleness that was his. I never did much with this boy when I had the chance. I missed his offer of friendship. I would not miss that offer if it were made today. His face would make sense to me today." (Willey 1999, pp.61-2)

We are also bad at spotting when peers are using us or when they might be "playing nice" in order to lead us into traps of bullying. In short, we are bad at spotting predators.

At this point, I should like to refer back to my "Briefly About" social languages. If you haven't read this, this would be a good time to do so. It should give you an understanding of why I think it matters to learn social skills, even if we cannot all learn to blend in perfectly, should we wish to. Any amount of skill in communicating who you are is better than none. Unfortunately, young neurotypical kid are not likely to all go out and learn how to communicate with us, so it is smart if we learn instead.

Keeping friends

For people on the spectrum, friendships take place under different terms than they do for others. Firstly, we tend to have few but very important friends, rather than many. This means that when we reach out to a friend, we often do not understand how or why they can be busy, and we may get jealous of their other friends if we feel neglected. These are difficult emotions to deal with when you are a child, and it is equally difficult to understand why our friend does not feel the same way.

We are exceptionally loyal friends, generally speaking, and often consider someone a close personal friend, even though we have perhaps grown apart. If they have ever been important to us, they will remain important for a very long time, even after an active friendship has ended.

And when it comes to how active a friendship is, this is where misunderstandings can easily occur. Because for us, it might very well be enough to spend one day a month with our best friend. We can also be on the other extreme, where we have to see them every day. So our friends can feel either neglected or not feel that the friendship is that close or important because we spend so little time cultivating and maintaining it, or they can feel absolutely suffocated by our attention.

As a parent, you can help to step in and guide us. If we are suffocating someone, try to make rules about how many times per week it is okay to call the same person, and how many times a month there should be playdates. If we are letting a potentially close friend become neglected, you can try to encourage us to call them or to socialize with them at school in some way.

Some will need relatively little guidance and others will need every minute detail explained and rehearsed. Social profiles and learning styles can be very different. Just be sure that you keep in mind the reason you are teaching and guiding your child. It should never be about making them "normal", but rather it should be about giving them ways to adapt to the world while retaining who they are in order to give them the best foundation for being happy.

The transition from child to teenager is where many problems in keeping friends can occur because the neurotypical peers will change their interests and behavior much earlier than we do. This is also when many experience bullying where we previously were more accepted. Jimmi wrote to me that:

"When I was little I did not want a lot of friends. It was the games that mattered. I had several friends to meet for playdates and my social needs were met completely. Later, in school, I made one really good friend, whom I saw more than the others. He also really liked hanging out with me. It was a great time. But in the teenage years it all started to change. Suddenly my really good friend also wanted to be with the "in" crowd. Our close friendship was waning. It was also in the teenage years that the bullying began and went on. I was bullied throughout my teenage years. I was an outsider and a loner, who missed having friends in general and felt very lonely. Today, as an adult, I have a few really good friends, and many acquaintances." (Jimmi, personal communication)

I included the last part of his email because I feel that it is important to add that though the teenage years can be so horribly lonely for many of us, we do find friendships again. Either in other people with ASD or simply once we find neurotypicals that are less judgmental. Our friends – the ones that last – are people who accept who we are, our difficulties and qualities, who take our social skills and sensory sensitivities into account, and who view us as equals.

Such people can be hard to find, both as a child and as an adult, but they are the only kind worth finding. My advice to both parents and children is that they are also worth looking for.

Number of friends

When it comes to the number of friends we have and the importance of that number, people on the spectrum generally fall into two categories, each at an extreme. Many are supremely happy with having one or two close friends, and sometimes, that can even be too much. On the other extreme are those to whom it is vitally important to have a great number of friends.

Usually, to those who want many friends, it is not deep personal friendships they are looking for. They want to be popular and well-liked, and they, as many neurotypicals do, measure their popularity by their number of friends. These children will usually speak of any person who is kind to them as a friend, and when they engage in social media, they will want everyone to accept friend requests – sometimes regardless of whether they know the person or not.

Again, here some guidance can be useful, but usually in the form of building a sense of identity and self-worth. This does not mean that they want these friends because they feel badly about themselves, but merely that ensuring a good self-worth and a well-defined sense of identity will help to shield these children against being hurt, socially. These children are the ones more likely to succumb to peer pressure, and if bullied, especially in a group setting, will respond very strongly and emotionally.

The children who are overwhelmed by a very low number of friends should be supported in keeping the friends they want to keep. You should also be ready to have a conversation or thirty if a friend moves away, becomes disinterested or if the children grow apart and the like.

For these children, their friends are people they feel safe with, and they will usually be the more socially reserved. They are not likely to call anyone new a friend because it takes a while to earn such a title.

They are less likely to care what others think and therefore less likely to succumb to peer pressure. This, unfortunately, also means they are quite likely to be bullied at some point during their school years.

But to these children, it is the opinions of their one or two friends that matter, and the few friends are more important to them than any number of acquaintances or online friends.

A different kind of friendship

One of the things that both parents and children have to accept is that, for the most part, the friendships we make, exist under a different set of circumstances than do friendships between neurotypical people.

Our ways of spending time together are often more structured or have a more specific purpose. Where others might just "meet up for coffee", we will instead meet to watch a certain television series or movie together, or as in my case, meet up and play a tabletop roleplaying game where we already know which game, which characters are played and who is going to be there.

Even if your child goes on to just "meet up for coffee" or "meet up for dinner", it is likely to be a very small number of people that they can do this with whilst feeling comfortable, or reasonably so.

We tend to be in the extremes when it comes to how often we see and speak to our friends. Either relatively rarely or every day. Some are perfectly content with not meeting people very often at all, and perhaps not even speaking very often. We are very different when it comes to this. A young woman with Asperger's wrote to me about the friendships she maintains and best feels she can cope with:

"I found out that I'm much better at maintaining friendships with boys [than with girls]. It's also mostly over Skype, with 2 or 3 of them, only meeting physically once in a while. It doesn't seem to be a problem that you don't speak to them for half or whole years, and then write once in a while when something happens within a common interest. It probably helps that most of them are also on the spectrum, or very well could be.
They aren't very close friendships in the typical sense, but it does prevent me from losing myself in the process. It seems to work because I can contact others when I actually have the energy to talk." (Signe, personal communication.)

When it comes to people we know well, our friends can become an anchor when we are in situations that make us anxious. For example, if we go to a movie in a new theater, a concert or perhaps a private party, the friend we have with us is the safety net. He/she will be the person we mostly speak to and they will be the person we arrive and leave with – especially if it is a party.

Alone is not lonely

This leads me to a question I am often asked by parents. Should you be worried if your child only has one friend? If they do not go out much? If they spend hours upon hours alone in their room?
No!
To a child on the spectrum, alone does not mean lonely. They are a far cry apart. As I talk about in the chapter "My room", we relish solitude and we need it. Some a lot more than others.

Quite often, a parent will have a very different view of their child's social needs and situation than does the child. Children and teenagers alike can be quite happy spending eight hours a day alone, while their parents are worried sick about their child's loneliness. Again, look at your child's profile and listen to what they say. Your child is not going to tell you that they feel happy with their friends and their lives if they are actually miserable and lonely. By far, the greatest number of people on the spectrum wouldn't even think of telling that lie, and a further immense number would be very obvious if they tried. Every person on the spectrum needs some amount of alone-time to function well. Some more, some less, but we all need it. And that is okay. We are not sad when we are alone. We are at peace, we are happy.

Need for playdates

As with the number of friends, parents often have a greater need for playdates than their children with ASD do. One playdate per month might be more than enough for your child, so do not worry about arranging several a week. It is unnecessary and stressful for your child, and it will not make them to learn social skills any faster; they have to do this at their own pace and desire.

However, as with anything else, I have to stress that we are all different, but that we tend to fall at the extremes. As for the need, desire and stamina for playdates, I want to demonstrate this difference by presenting quotes from two girls:

"It's hard to get friends so I appreciate the ones I have. But it's easy getting playdates. I'm tired after having friends over but I can go to school the day after. I like having three or four playdates a week, sometimes five. Sometimes it's the same friend and sometimes different ones." (Anonymous, personal communication.)

"I don't have energy for playdates on school days. I want to and I also have fun while playing, but I am completely drained for three days afterwards. Luckily, my parents know this and they are good at arranging my week so I can handle it all." (Rebecca, personal communication)

Who to invite

You cannot choose your child's friends for them. They know who they like and who they do not, and trying to match them with children you think would be good for them is not going to work. Playdates should be with the children that your child already likes or is interested in knowing and playing with.

Activity

For the most part, the children your child will want to play with are ones with similar interests or who have the patience to at least put up with a certain game for some amount of time. This means that the activities that will be engaged in during playdates will for the most part be the things your child already likes to do.

Do not try to force a new game onto your child because they are playing with in a social context rather than alone, because if they are not prepared, they will not understand why you are doing this, and they may very easily become frustrated.

It is not really that hard though, because the children that are friends with your child already know who they are and what they like; usually from school or another such environment, so they can somewhat easily adapt to the situation. Very often, the children's games will consist in being together about a normally solitary activity, or being parallel in a solitary activity, such as Legos or computer games.

This can and will probably be the solution far into the teen years, and sometimes even as adults. Luckily, playing computer and console games is no longer a strange hobby, it is something almost everyone does to some extent.

Time frame for playdates

Consider how much energy your child spends on being social and how they feel in general at the time. Are they extra stressed out, for example, because of a new teacher, the color of the neighbor's fence having been changed or a family birthday that is coming up?

Consider also which days you invite children over. On school days, most children and adolescents with ASD are so exhausted they can hardly see straight, so those are bad days to add something extra to their schedule. So keep it to weekends unless you have a fair idea that your child can cope, and keep the playdate to an amount of time that allows your child to recharge in time for next week. Also, for us, simply having a time-frame can be important. Signe, who has Asperger's, wrote to me about her playdates:

"I was known for wanting to control the games when I was little. When I had a playdate, it had to happen according to my head. I got angry if it did not happen the way I thought it should, or I did not know what to do if my friend got me to do something else. I also wanted to play the same thing over and over. I don't remember how long my playdates lasted. But I remember that I always used to think 'When are they going home?' or 'When is it okay for me to leave?' Not because I did not want to be there, but it would have given me a sense of calm if there had been a set time for the playdate to end." (Signe, personal communication.)

BULLYING

Bullying is not just an issue that most aspies meet at some point in their lives. In most of our childhoods and youths, it is a fact of life. What most people fail to understand, is that the others do not have to hit you to hurt you. In many cases they will physical hurt you, but in many others (especially for female aspies), it is done with words and social exclusion. Much could be written about different forms of bullying and the effects it can have. I will focus on some types of bullying and effects that are more common for children on the spectrum, and the ways the child or teenager might think.

Who can bully, and how?

We used to define bullying mostly as a physical act between peers but these days, we acknowledge different forms of bullying, and also that the bully is not necessarily a peer of the victim. I would like to form a picture that can help you to see how one can be victimized and by whom.

Bullying can, of course, take a physical form which, at least for the most part, can be seen by bystanders, and which may leave physical marks on the body. Another form of bullying is social exclusion. It may sound relatively harmless: "The other kids just do not want to play with you..." But there is a difference between other children not taking an interest, and actively excluding you. The exclusion is very obvious, and it is made to be obvious to the victim by the bully or – as is more often the case – bullies. It is intended to be hurtful, and even though some children on the spectrum do not respond to this type of bullying – mostly due to their lack of Theory of Mind skills – many others do, and are very hurt by this. Emotional bullying is very often connected to both of the two former types mentioned. This takes the form of ridicule and humiliation. Most often, this is done by a group, and the feeling of humiliation intensifies the more public the bullying is, especially when no one takes your side or attempts to protect you.

So, who can bully your child? You might think it is probably just other kids you have to worry about. I am very sorry to tell you that while your child's peers will make up the vast majority of probable bullies, there are examples of teachers and other adults in similar positions of authority participating actively in bullying. This can take the form of humiliating the child in front of peers or making statements privately to the child that are cruel and intended to cause anxiety.

There can be a degree of bullying from family members. In addition to the aforementioned types of bullying, family members can torment a child by dismissing their handicaps and/or diagnoses, actively provoking, for example, sensory sensitivities - sometimes in the genuine belief that the child is making it up and wanting them to admit it or stop being "difficult", other times in the erroneous belief that this will de-sensitize the child to the sensory experience.

A newer form of bullying which has arisen with the internet, chat rooms, forums, social media and with children having their own phones, is cyber-bullying. What makes this exceptionally damaging for the victim, is that there is no escape. With the other forms of bullying, you have a break once you are home. School might be hell, but at least you can leave.

When your tormenters are with you constantly - via text, social media, online computer and console games - you have no place to run or hide. This means you are constantly confronted with your tormenters, and even if you block them, they can make new accounts to continue their harassment, if they are persistent enough. Cyber-bullying can take several forms. It can be done directly, by sending harmful messages, posting status updates or comments that are intended to hurt, but it can also be done in other, less direct ways, for example, by impersonating someone – which is more easily done than you might imagine, or by doc-dropping/doxing someone. Doc-dropping is when someone posts personal information such as telephone numbers, addresses or other means of directly contacting their target. Most often, several pieces of information are put out simultaneously. Videos intended to embarrass can be also taken and posted on various sites.

There are, unfortunately, quite a lot of suicides directly connected with this form of bullying, which makes it all the more important to teach your child to protect themselves online: Do not give out personal information, only give your username to close friends, block people who harass you and do this quickly. Take screenshots of abusive or harassing messages, including the usernames of those who wrote it, save these and file them. Keep evidence in case you need it later.

Keep in mind that if an adult is involved, it is called cyber-harassment or cyber-stalking, and different laws will apply. You can research this online and I recommend starting with sites like stopcyberbullying.org

(Side-note to this section: Because many children and teenagers with ASD are more easily manipulated than others, they may be manipulated into taking revealing photos or video and be victims of a phenomenon called revenge porn. This is a heavy and complicated topic, and I recommend you do research online, check legislation in your country, as well as speak to your child about the risks associated with other people possessing images of you and do this a few years before the age at which you might worry something could happen. Your child will need extended processing time, they will have many questions, and they will have to be prepared for what to do and what not to do, in case the situation does arise.

WHAT YOUR CHILD WITH ASPERGER'S WANTS YOU TO KNOW

If anyone does manipulate your child before the age of 18, it will fall under child pornography laws. In this case, be aware that depending on the country you live in, your child can actually be charged with the crime as well, having taken pictures of themselves and possessing them!)

Emotions and their consequences

As you will know from the section about the Amygdala and Emotions, we have a tendency to feel in extremes, so if we feel humiliated or afraid, we do it to such a degree that we cannot calm ourselves down, much less think rationally. It also means that once our buttons have been pushed, other children will see these, because we do not have the capability to hide it so as to protect ourselves. This means that we are a perfect target for bullies. Our buttons are worn on our sleeves, we are socially naive and we react strongly to being teased and bullied. This is everything they want in a victim. (I do not mean to ascribe them any more cruelty or evil than children actually possess, but victim is the correct word for a child who is bullied the way many of us are.)

Due to the emotional reaction we have, our way of thinking can quickly be affected and combined with the child's profile this can decide any number of more or less permanent ways of viewing the world and others in it.

There are two basic reactions to being bullied. Externalizing and internalizing. Neither of these patterns of reaction are more or less "self-absorbed" or "ego-centric" than the other. Everyone has one of the other to some extent, people with ASD simply have more difficulty regulating emotions, and therefore whichever reaction comes out stronger and more dramatically.

Externalization

As humans we have three basic, instinctual reactions to threats. Fight, flight or freeze. Externalizers are fighters, yet instead of hurting the people who they feel threatened by, they may very well break or throw objects. This might happen once rage or anger, often propelled fear mostly, can no longer be contained within them, and instincts take over. Rationality is long gone, and the best thing is to remove the threat. However, be cautious of leaving the child alone as their lashing out can overlap with internalization. Reacting outwardly can become about hurting oneself as well. For example, they may slam their hand or head on something, sometimes to the degree of actually causing damage to themselves, especially since the child may not have the reflex to stop when something hurts.

The externalization can also evolve into direct attacks on the people who are hurting them. This may happen especially if the child has concluded that the bullies are predators, monsters or enemies, rather than "people".

The lack of trust which, initially, is reserved for the bullies or "enemies" can also expand into becoming a general state of emotion for the child. They will react to several groups then; the "primary bullies" or "active bullies", the "secondary bullies", who are the active followers who participate but do not initiate, the "passive followers", who watch, maybe laugh a little, but do not directly participate in the bullying, and lastly the "silent majority", the people who watch or know about the bullying, but do nothing to stop it.

In the case of this last group, I am reminded of the famous quote attributed to Edmund Burke; "The only thing necessary for the triumph of evil is for good men to do nothing."

This is the line of thinking that might cause the child to lash out against the silent majority as well.

Teachers can fall into these categories, as well. If the child feels that the teachers know and do nothing, or that perhaps they even participate, this can cause a great distrust not only of peers, but also of authority figures.

This lack of trust can have a domino effect, expanding suddenly to include almost everyone so the child has taught themselves that no one cares. These children thus have or develop a tendency toward being distrustful, toward angry and violent reactions, and sometimes toward arrogance. A type of thinking where it is assumed with certainty that everyone else is wrong.

For these children, taking the Emotion Toolbox and Cat-kit into use can have great benefit.

Note that the outward reaction displayed by some children and teenagers with ASD is not simply anger, but an agitated externalized depression. This term is applied to depressions which are expressed through anger, violence, consciously behaving badly and possibly engaging with a harmful social crowd. It is a relatively new term, and research is still being done. In this case, fixing the behavior of anger and violence will not solve the problem. You will need to look into the causes of the depression. Again I recommend the Emotion Toolbox and Cat-kit.

Internalization
The child who internalizes has a higher risk of unfortunate reactions to traumatic life events, whether these occur in childhood or later. With the "internalizer", one needs to watch out for depression, anxiety, problems with self-esteem and self-worth, eating disorders, self-harm and potential suicide attempts.

Most people think of depression and any of these other problems as things that affect teenagers and adults, so I want to make this very clear; Children can experience clinical depression too. I, myself, had my first major depression when I was seven. It lasted for three years, and included serious considerations of suicide for almost the entire duration.

Depression, anxiety and suicidal thoughts can occur from a very young age, and I very much doubt that others, younger than me, have not had the same thoughts. The younger your child is when first experiencing these thoughts and feelings, the more difficult it is, as they might think, as I did, that it is normal to think and feel this way. And it does indeed become normal after a while. So they might not, as I did not, tell anyone about their thoughts and feelings. Impairments or delays in the Theory of Mind department also have influence here.

So, what are the inner thoughts of an internalizer? "Why me? It is always me. There is something wrong with me, or they would also pick on others. I am alone. No one will help me. They always want to hurt me".

These children might experience a sort of paranoia of peers and may assume that peers always have bad intent towards them.

The low self-esteem and self-worth will in some cases be noticeable, but in others, they may know enough about acting to be able to pretend to be okay, so as to not worry a parent – especially if they feel the parent already has enough to deal with. The same goes for depression and suicidal thoughts.

Self-harm and eating disorders usually do not begin until the teen years, but it is possible to see it in children as well, however, an eating disorder in a child is not necessarily a result of bullying, but can be a sign of other things; see chapter about Food, section on Eating Disorders.

Thoughts that can deter suicide attempts

If your child suffers from suicidal thoughts, it is important that they have other thoughts to keep them from actually trying. Whether the suicidal thoughts are constant or come only during "depression attacks" (like anxiety attacks, a more or less sudden and intense experience which passes in either minutes, hours or a day's time), there needs to be something that blocks the child from acting on the thought.

This is one of the areas in which conventional methods may not work, and you need to consider your child's ASD profile. Once again I suggest consulting with a specialized professional.

Some of the thought categories that work for people on the spectrum are:

- The effects on family/animals of my being gone. Here it is thoughts like "Who will feed the dog?" or "My parents will be very sad."

- Missing an exciting experience. Perhaps a new movie is coming out, or a trip to a place that has to do with a special interest. It can be things that seem completely trivial but having some experience ahead that is interesting and exciting can be the thought that leads to the "Not today" conclusion.

- Not solving the problem. This one can be understood in two ways. If the child is working on a project of some kind, there can be a desire to finish it. The other is this; "Suicide does not solve the problem of how I ended up feeling this way. The problem wins if I die." This is a more complex thought that requires the child to have a certain profile. Many others will think of suicide as the solution to the problem, rather than something to overcome, so this way of thinking may not work, though it does for some.

- Fear of not succeeding. Strangely, this is one of the most common thoughts. There is a tendency to think of the prospect of failing to die as something shameful. It is worse than not trying at all. Also, fear of pain may keep them from using a knife, and fear of being found and stopped could keep them from trying things like pills. This brings me to firearms. Even though firearms do not provide a sure way of dying, children may think they do, and therefore be more likely to try. This is why I recommend keeping firearms away from the home if your child is prone to depression. If possible, I recommend living somewhere where firearms are difficult to get. Mind you, this recommendation is in regard to children and young people who are prone to depression and suicidal thoughts, not people with ASD in general.

- The special interest. It can function as a distraction at times where you would not think anything could. If at all possible, I would keep something that concerns the child's special interest near or on their person at all times. Something they can see, touch, smell or hear. If they love Batman, it can be a figurine in their pocket, which they can grab and hold. If they love a certain song or movie, make sure they have it on a device with them, along with headphones. Make sure it is charged – they may forget that detail. Try your best to schedule things that have to do with the interest at regular intervals, and make sure the child knows when it is.

CHORES

It is good for children to participate in the home. It makes them feel accomplished (especially if complimented and rewarded), included and "grown up". But there is a big difference in which instructions to give to a child with ASD, compared to one who is not on the spectrum.

Most of the problems one will encounter here, are problems that arise due to delayed or decreased executive functions. I mention these in the "Briefly About" cognitive abilities.

It is important that you understand that your child is not stupid or rebellious, it is simply that their brain processes information differently, and that their ability to govern prioritizing, planning, time management and impulse control is inhibited, and that they need tools and good instructions from you to avoid this becoming a problem.

The language barrier

"Would you take out the trash?" is a turn of phrase you would expect most children to understand. But if you live with someone on the spectrum, especially someone who is not aware and has not been taught to understand this phrase in the way it is meant, you are most likely to hear a "yes" or "no" answer, and then the trash will stay exactly where it was. Why? Because we understand what is said, not what is meant. We will either be confused by the question because it lacks a description of the specific circumstances under which we would or would not take out the trash, and therefore we cannot answer. Alternatively, we will make up the rest of the question ourselves, the most likely of which would be "Would you take out the trash, if I asked you to?" to which we then either answer "yes" or "no", but you still have not actually asked directly and so no action takes place.

This problem of understanding will continue until the person with ASD has learned to understand such phrases – yet do not expect that once we have learned one, we have learned them all. It does not work that way, unfortunately. Even if the question is understood, a teenager with ASD may still rebel, in which case you are most likely to get the "no" answer.

The way around this is to learn how "aspie-logic" and the "aspie-language" works, and to work with it rather than against it. Instead of asking "Would you...?", you can say "I need you to... before..." or "...because..."

Fill in the blanks, it can be anything. What is important here is that you have stated what you would like them to do and before what time. Optimally, there should be several reminders if it is not a standing agreement. Also, consider that your child may need to be told a very specific time for when to do things, otherwise they may get confused or have a very hard time making the choice for when to do it – even within a relatively short time frame. It depends on how ASD affects your child. Doing chores is a routine that needs to be built and maintained like any other. There should be clear instructions on what to do and preferably you should show the child how to do it the first few times and then watch them do it, so there is no doubt as to the scope of the chore.

Include details in the description and if your child is good at listening to explanations, then do so as you are show ing it. Otherwise, write it down in detail. If there are many steps then make a list of which order things should be done in so you eliminate any possible confusion, which may otherwise lead to feelings of inferiority and subsequently to meltdowns. It is also usually good for the child to have a chart to check off once the chore is completed. This will give a sense of achievement. When you check the box, you are done, and you can feel good about having helped out.

Visual and written instructions

If we have never done something before, we can have a hard time following verbal instructions, especially if these are given before the task is performed, rather than during. There are things you can do to teach your child autonomy in performing a task at home, and you can be quite sure that it will be done in the exact same way every time. For example, write it down for us, step by step. This should be done in a point or list form, in the correct order. Do not leave anything out. Include every detail that matters to the task being completed correctly. If your child has a hard time following the instructions, it usually means they are not detailed or concrete enough. Another good way to teach your child a task is to show them. This does not necessarily mean that you should leave out the written instructions, it is good to combine the two.

Do the task you want your child to do while they watch, and tell them what you are doing – with as few extra words as possible. If you are showing them how to wring out a cloth, for example, do it first, and let them feel how wet it should be for doing this particular task. If you have taught them to wipe off dust, and you now want to teach them to wash a floor, the cloth is different, and how wet it should be is also different. Show them the difference, do not expect them to know.

After you have shown them, watch them do it. Make it a moment of teaching, not a "I'm-watching-to-make-sure-you-can-do-it-right"-thing. They should not be afraid of making a mistake when you are watching. Once they have the routine down, let them do it on their own.

Rigid thinking

An element of the ASD mind is rigid thinking; the 'one track mind'. This means that once we are doing something, it can be very easy to keep going, forgetting everything else. It also means that if there is a set of instructions to follow to do a task, and something makes it impossible to follow said instructions, we get struck. We simply do not know what to do. For example, if you keep a certain brand of a cleaning product for cleaning the sink and you have shown your child how to clean the sink with it, but if the brand changes the look of the product, or you switch to a different product, you may have to let your child know again which product to use. If the tools for a task are relocated, or you get a new one, your child will have to learn again which tools to use and how. It will take time for them to adjust to the new tool because it might be longer or shorter or feel different to the touch. If it is a vacuum cleaner, it might sound different.

The order and the way in which things are done, and the way of doing it cannot change. Your child has learnt to do this chore in this way using these products and tools in that order.

This also means there is no quick way to fold laundry or wash the dishes. It will be done right, or it will not be done at all.

Likewise, if you send them shopping, the shopping list might say "butter", but not which kind. If the store is out of the usual brand of butter, or even packaging and particular size of package, your child may get stuck and not know what to do. They will not think to just get a different size or brand. If you send them for fresh potatoes and there are none, your child may very well get stuck as well. They will not be likely to consider frozen goods as an alternative, so it will be good to specify alternatives that are acceptable or instruct them to call home if there is a problem. These types of conversations with your child will help teach them to think in alternatives and to problem-solve.

Sensory Sensitivities

With regard to the type of chores your child does around the home, please remember that they may have sensory sensitivities with, for example, vacuum cleaners, as it is not uncommon for the sound to hurt our ears. Likewise, the sound of other household machines may be an issue, or the smell of particular cleaning products. The tactile feeling of certain types of cloths or wearing rubber gloves may be disturbing to a point that you either need to find a different solution, or not assign this particular chore to your child. Please take this into account when choosing which chores to assign to your child. They should feel included and valued, not punished. They may become less sensitive to something as they age, but it may also continue to be a problem through adulthood. If you do not see it changing in their teens, you may want to search for other ways for them to do said chore, in order to help prepare them for living on their own.

SCHOOL PARTIES & BIRTHDAYS

I realize that a parent hopes that their child will enjoy having many friends and having friends over for birthday parties. A parent might also very well hope that they can drop off their child at a classmate's birthday party knowing that when they come back to pick their child up, they will have had a good time.

None of this is to be expected when your child had ASD.

Let us assume that your child has not experienced bullying, and that their classmates are, if not understanding, then at least accepting of your child and the differences in behavior from themselves. Their parents will not know the extent to which your child can or cannot participate, their eating habits etc. Your child's friend's parents do not know your child's autism. They may have some general knowledge of autism, and they might know something about your child, specifically, but they do not know it all, and you cannot prepare them properly, though you can do your very best.

Birthday party games and play

Whether it is a competition of eating a string candy the fastest, balancing an egg on a spoon while racing, or jumping in a sack, kids make up games, and parents make up games that kids are expected to all participate in during these events. And often they are likely to either involve motor skills or food. Your child may either be the very best at these (because by coincidence or planning, they cater to their specific skill-set), or the very worst. It is likely to be the latter, due to the tendency for us to have issues with regard to these very areas. This will perhaps sound petty and immature, but one less positive characteristic about people with ASD is that if we understand the concepts of competition, winning and losing, we tend to really hate losing.

Because of the way we understand language, we are very likely to be of the opinion (and very strongly so), that second place means you have also lost. Everything that is not winning is, by definition, losing. People who lose are often made fun of in contexts we have seen (even if we have not been victims of it), and so we do not want to be those people. In our minds, not being good at something, no matter how silly that something is, can seem like defeat. So many of us can react quite badly to not being good at things the very first time we try them. So when we lose, we have to control ourselves tightly not to throw a fit, which is something we do not want to do, because it is embarrassing. But having poor self-control, as children do, this can be extremely difficult, and if we succeed at all, we will have used up a lot of energy on this one task. This can all be avoided of course, if your child has learnt that not winning is okay, and that it is all in good fun. Some can learn this easily, and some never do, and even when they know it intellectually, the emotional side can still override the attempts to control behavior. If this is the case, simply find ways to avoid such games. (This would also include sports competitions and board games.)

A bully/teaser present

One is much worse than the other, of course. There are gradients here, but the essence of the problem is the same. Someone is present whom you want to get away from, but you cannot get away. This is a situation which, as someone who has experienced bullying, I would try to avoid at any and all costs. I would rather not have had any birthday parties, and not attended anyone else's birthday party if going meant I would be stuck in a situation with a bully. I already had to endure them at school, but outside? That was too much to ask.

Yet I was not given the option, due to the culture in my country, which dictates that you are supposed to invite everyone from your class (usually around 25 kids), or at least everyone of the same gender.

I would advise, on behalf of your child, to give them an option. If you know they are being bullied or teased, and that the offending child will be present, try to provide your child with a way out. If they have to go to the party, make sure they can call to be picked up with relatively short notice. If they are having the party, try to find some way to avoid that child is present. For example, if the bully is of the opposite gender, can you then invite only the same gender? If the bully is the same gender, consider either only inviting the children that are your child's friends (regardless of school and grade), or not having a party at all.

Talk to your child about options, and ask what they prefer. Try to have all options mapped out, including reasons why you have excluded other options. Explain it all in an age- and maturity-appropriate manner.

And all the usual suspects

As with everything else, the issues of sensory sensitivities and social exhaustion threaten to ruin it all. Try to take these into account, which, of course, is most easily done if you are hosting. But if your child is attending someone else's party, try contacting their parents and discuss with them what to do. Let them know what your main concerns are when it comes to, for example, sensory sensitivities – you do not have to talk about diagnoses or use the correct terms, you can use vaguer terms or even white lies – and if you have time, offer assistance; "My child really dislikes strawberries, so if you plan to put those in the cake, would it be okay if I brought one without?" or "My child is allergic to strawberries, they make him/her very ill. If they are in the cake, would it be okay if...."

If your child's diagnosis is known by classmates or parents, or if you are comfortable with it, try to discuss the option of your child going to sit in a quiet room to have breaks from the social events.

Also, try to make sure your child can escape the party quickly if needed. Either give them the option to call for you, or discuss with the hosting parents if they would be okay with you hanging out during the party, again you could suggest that you assist if you think they will not be offended by the offer.

There are children with ASD who have no issue with these situations. Again, it all depends on the profile of the child, and what they focus on in those situations. Signe, who has Asperger's, wrote a great example of this to me:

"I always attended school parties and birthdays. I wanted to go to the school parties, because I like dancing to loud music. Unfortunately, I did not like the music they played, and when I suggested any of the metal or Celtic music I liked, I was ignored. Birthdays weren't awful, so far as I remember them. There was candy and soda (which I was very focused on as a child), and fun games, so I had fun even though I wasn't a part of the other children's groups." (Signe, personal communication.)

Some children will focus so much on a certain aspect that it all becomes acceptable or even enjoyable. I, personally, relate to wanting to dance to loud music, and due to that, being comfortable at school parties. It may also be that the child having a birthday party has a really nice dog, or they have a good swing in the yard. If this is what your child focuses on in those situations, do not ruin it by telling them they cannot play with the dog or whatever it is. Try bargaining with them, and make deals with the other parents. They can play with the dog for twenty minutes, for example.

HOBBIES & EXTRACURRICULAR ACTIVITIES

As with any other child, a certain amount of hobbies or extracurricular activities can be very healthy but having a child with ASD, it might be hard to know which environments are productive and which can be problematic.

Energy

Always consider how much energy is left after school. And consider mental and physical energy apart from each other. They might be very mentally tired, but can still benefit from some form of physical activity. It is also possible that your child's level of energy seems more than it is, simply because they are so excited about what they are going to do. In this case, it will most likely backfire in the evening or the following day.

This is a trial and error thing, I know, but it is worth trying to figure out.

What sort of hobby?

What I want to do is different from what the other kids want to do. And on the off-chance that my interest is considered normal, it will still be extreme in focus. I might love horses, but that does not mean I want to go riding twice a week; it means I want to go every day, and for much longer than other kids do. Your child is more likely to have hobbies or special interests like chess, science, computer games, foreign languages, specific historical periods and the like. Even if others perceive it as odd, something about this appeals to your child and the way they think. If you want to understand why this particular thing is so exciting for them, talk to them, ask them about it. They will be so happy to tell you why their hobby or interest is the best thing in the world. Other children and adults may not understand and may react to it, and it is very important that you try to find the positive in their interests when others don't, in order to provide your child with social and emotional support. You may also have to explain to your child why other children are not as interested in the history of stamps as they are. It can be very confusing to someone so young, why we are so different from everyone else, and why they don't like the things we like. Again, the delayed Theory of Mind skills are at play.

Team sports vs. Solo sports

Children with ASD very rarely do well in certain types of team sports – yet there are exceptions!

Football, basketball, handball and that type of game is usually not the answer to getting your child some physical exercise. Generally speaking, sports that include balls, either throwing or kicking, are not our kinds of sports. And the team mates (and opponent team mates) will notice this quickly. Will Hadcroft wrote of his experience:

"I was frightened of the other boys, and this was very apparent to them. Tackling was a nightmare, and I let the ball go without much of a fight, to the fury of my fellow team members" (Hadcroft 2005, p.62).

Very often, good types of sports for us are things like martial arts (karate, kendo, thai chi, aikido etc.) – as very often there will be some level of interest in the culture and history attached to this, or gymnastics, solo dancing and swimming. Less physical types of exercise, can be just as useful in terms of meditative quality, for example, shooting, both guns and bows, because a great deal of concentration is required, and usually there is a somewhat long period between each shot. There is also a lot of focus on breathing, hand-eye coordination etc. All in all, it can be extremely mentally beneficial.

"Training martial arts is very helpful in a number of ways. For one, the training is highly structured and you are told which technique to practice at what time. In most forms there are also clear rules for social interaction. In the Japanese martial art Aikido, for example, the hierarchy is clear from the belt colors and within belt colors experience decides the rank. If you are ever in doubt about anything social, the rule is to ask your senior in rank, and since they have more experience they will often know. If they do not know they will ask their senior and so on. There is only one master, and if there are any matters to be settled he or she will decide. Apart from the social rules being more clear than in other places, it is also a great way to have physical interaction with other people in a safe setting. And obviously you will learn ways to defend yourself which actually builds your self-esteem and thereby lowers your anxiety in situations of threat as you now know you have "weapons" to defend yourself with should it become necessary. I have, personally, also found that having an interest in a particular martial art in common can bring about some good friendships over time - something which may not come easy to many of us." (Sif, personal communication)

Non-sport activities
Other activities that are highly beneficial and that we are likely to be or become good at are, for example, chess and music. Again, a high level of concentration and forethought is required. In music, good fine motor skills are required to attain any professional skill level, but whether this is achieved or not, the playing of and interaction with music, in itself, can be beneficial.

Drama classes are also often a great joy. Naturally, it is mostly those who enjoy mimicking and mirroring behavior that are attracted to this activity. But drama classes and roleplaying are both great activities for teaching social skills and Theory of Mind skills.

For most of us, Lego is an unparalleled joy for either a short or long period of time. There is something about building something, the planning, thinking out of details and creating a scene. Generally speaking, it is the building part that is important. Once we are done building, we do not tend to play so much afterwards, if at all.

When we get a little older – or when we are allowed computer access – we quickly find our way to games like Minecraft and the Sims. Once again, it is mainly the building part we are interested in.

Whatever appeals to us, it does so for a reason, and should not be downplayed as "just a hobby". For us, it is these "hobbies" that bring us joy, that allow us to think, build and create.

Benefits in adulthood

Every hobby, interest or activity brings us something while we are engaged in it, but they also teach us things that can be brought into adulthood. Martial arts and meditative activities, for example, swimming and dancing, bring body awareness and a better ability to control our focus, they also give tools to control emotional reactions in situations where this is needed.

Lego, Minecraft, Sims and the like allow us to fine-tune our attention to detail and indulge in it. This is a great skill for many jobs, and through learning to use it skillfully rather than being disturbed by it - though it might at times be annoying for us to live with - we may also learn the concept that the same attribute can have two values simultaneously, thus leading us into the world of thinking in nuance.

All of this can be guided, and you have the opportunity to do this. This is to say, rather than thinking that our interests are silly or strange, think of how they help us to hone our skills for the future, and support them.

SPECIAL INTERESTS

Other people have hobbies, people with ASD also have special interests. We can also have hobbies, but mostly we find certain things that are so interesting to us that the closest word to describing it would be "obsession".

They are interests that give us such joy that it can be hard to convince us to do anything else.

The first special interest can show itself at a very early age or not appear until late teens or early adulthood. Some people have only one for their whole lifetime. Others lose interest over time – anywhere from months to years to decades – and pick up a new one. Yet others seem to collect special interests. They rarely, if ever, lose an interest, but continue to gain them. This version can be very frustrating to the person with ASD. They want to give time to all their interests, and having to prioritize between them can be difficult, emotionally. You want to give them all equal time, which is impossible, and you feel guilty about engaging in one interest because it means you are neglecting another.

It should be noted that, although rare, some do not have special interests at all.

Gender differences

As with many other things, there is a tendency to have certain expressions of ASD depending on gender, but as always, you should never expect your child to follow any norm or prediction. Stay open to any trait being expressed differently in your child.

Generally speaking, people with the classic or "male" profile tend to have interests that are odd in focus as well as intensity. Examples could be air traffic, collecting batteries, or ancient Sumerian history... things that not too many people find fascinating.

People with the "female" profile tend to have interests that are more common in focus but obsessive in intensity. Boy bands, fashion, popular book series – what you will find is that while the interest is the same as that of peers, the person with ASD will know much more about the subject and spend much more time on it. Some professionals tend to divide more firmly into these profiles, but it should be noted that someone can have a profile that allows for both types of special interests. Special interests can also involve much more than collecting objects or knowledge. Sometimes they involve creating things: Sculptures, paintings, drawings, music or things more uncommon.

Enjoyment

One of the important components of a special interest is the enjoyment we experience when engaging in it. It can be so all-encompassing that we forget everything else. All the bad experiences of our day, all negative thoughts, all worries disappear, and we are inside the world of the special interest. Whether this is music, fiction or trains, the enjoyment is the same. In terms of enjoyment, the special interest is much more than a hobby. It is not something we just like to do, it is what makes life worth living. For this reason, taking away the special interest should never, and I do mean never, be used as punishment. Taking it away can trigger deep despair beyond what is healthy for a child to experience.

However, extended access to the special interest can be used as a reward system. If, for example, the child normally has access for two hours per day, a reward for completing homework might be an extra 15 or 30 minutes.

As a side note to this, if you see your child losing the enjoyment of their special interest, paired with any depressive symptom, if it no longer makes them happy and is not replaced by a new one, this should be cause for concern regarding their mental health, especially if depression is already a concern, or they have previously had suicidal thoughts.

Thought blocker

When it comes to depression and anxiety, the special interest can be a very effective thought blocker. As previously mentioned, all negative thoughts can cease while engaged in the special interest, as we are so consumed with immersing ourselves in the interest and the joy it brings. In this sense, it can easily be used as a method to reduce anxiety and even to treat depression, although medication may be needed as well. Consider it working in the way that it takes up all the space in our brains and focuses us completely. So there is no room for thoughts concerning what happened in school, or the prospect of tomorrow being stressful. Everything is about the interest during the time we engage in it. Ellen describes how the television show Doctor Who did this for her;

"Some might say that special interests are a hindrance, and though this can be true to some extent, they're mostly a positive thing. When I was depressed and bullied at school, the thought of coming home to watch Doctor Who helped me get through the day." (Ellen, personal communication)

Energizer

While most other things drain our energy, the special interest is a great restorative. Aside from sleep and solitude, it can be the only way to truly recharge, and combined with solitude, it is incomparable. That being said, it should be noted that some special interests can simultaneously drain energy as well. There is nothing to do about this, as we cannot force ourselves to have a different interest. I merely point it out to make parents aware of it.

If the interest is a computer game with a social aspect, for example, World of Warcraft, Eve or another MMORPG, the social aspect will be draining to some degree, just as computer games that have timers or require fast action in some way can also drain energy. The result is that while energy overall is still restored by engaging in the interest, it may not be as quick as with a previous interest, or it may restore energy in the form of making the child happy, but the social capacity has been completely filled. In such cases, I suggest consulting with an ASD professional to find solutions for optimal energy restoration during the time spent on the interest. This can include tools to make the social aspects of the game easier, giving the child reading material on the game (like stories about it if they like a roleplaying aspect of it, or blogs with tips for improving game skills), or perhaps having the child write about what they have done and achieved in the game.

In the last case, I highly suggest not to post such writings online. Do not add yet another social component by posting blogs or videos, as the child is then likely to encounter criticism online, or "trolls", which are people who make a hobby of writing mean things to get responses from their victims.

If your child writes a diary or story about their game, keep it amongst friends and family, and if they want you or others to read it, your commentary should be positive and encouraging at all times – remember, you are commenting on the topic that makes your child the happiest, and the happiness and enjoyment connected with this interest is vital for their mental health.

Your child can be extra vulnerable to criticism or negative statements about the topic of their interest, therefore, it is important to always keep a positive tone when discussing it.

Sense of identity

Your child's special interest can be a great part of their sense of identity. They may use terms in a similar way to adults describing themselves as doctors or teachers when asked who they are.

I am a role-player, for example, and I identify with this term just as much as with the term aspie. It is a part of what makes you who you are, and you feel like a part of a group, just knowing that there are others with this same interest who identify in the same way. This also means that if there is a gap between two special interests, or even if one is gained and after some time, the old one is lost, there can be an identity crisis. If I lost interest in role playing games, I could suddenly no longer say that I am a role-player, and this would mean there was a "gap" in the list of terms and adjectives that I use to describe myself.

It can therefore be a very good idea to have a talk about this if it is relevant. Talk about how the experience gained during the time engaging in an interest is still a part of who they are, and that even if there is no longer a simple term for it, they could call themselves a "former role-player" or a "former train enthusiast". This means they can still appreciate having had this interest, and everything they learned from it.

Talk about how identity evolves as you grow older, and how this is good and normal and nothing to be concerned about

Possibilities of employment

Some interests are exceptionally useful, both in terms of gaining skills and knowledge to ease your life, but also in terms of finding a job. Interests such as computer programming can lead to very well paid jobs very early in life because the person with ASD will teach themselves the skill they are interested in from an early age. Other interests that can lead to employment in adulthood may include psychology, engineering, design, paleontology and many more. Even an interest in seemingly "useless" things may lead to a long term job. I mention this because there is a tendency for parents to ask me how to make their children interested in things that they can actually use later in life. Unfortunately, as I mentioned before, there is no way to force an interest, but there are many ways to steer in a direction that is employable – but you may have to think somewhat out of the box.

POCKET MONEY

When it comes to money, several different difficulties can arise. As often seen, they are of varying severity, and some can overlap.

Conceptualizing the value of money

This is difficult for many children, if not most. For someone with ASD, money can be such a vague idea that we have no clue what to do with it. The main problem is that we cannot properly visualize money, or grasp the concept of how much something is worth and why.

This is especially true in this age of credit cards and internet/phone transfers. This may result lack of control of money as an adult, massive debt and overspending combined with no clear idea of the consequences, which means that the consequences sometimes are very dire indeed before we realize there even is a problem. And then we have to learn very quickly to control money, and to do so under problematic circumstances.

Teach your child about money. Use cash, not just numbers written down; we might be able to understand such numbers, but for many, they do not truly hit home. Introduce your child to concepts of budgeting. It does not have to be a full budget, of course, but when they have a small amount of pocket-money, talk to them about how much it is and what can be bought with it. Talk to them about what could be bought with twice as much or ten times as much, thereby introducing the concept and idea of saving for something, and then discuss the concept of saving money for next week or even just tomorrow, and the benefits of that. This could be done by playing a pretend game, in which they use their money to buy a number of edible items that they really enjoy, for example, candy or fruit. Have the physical money present for the game, and make drawings representing purchases and items, or if you have the items they want to buy with their money, have those present. Have them pretend to spend all of their money buying candy or fruit, and then discuss what will happen if they eat it all now, or if they save some food or luxury (candy) for later. Then play the game where they only spend, for example, half of their money, or a quarter of it. Talk about how much money they have left and what they could do with it.

When they are older, introduce concepts of rent, paying for electricity and water, paying for phones and internet, so as to prepare them for the expenses paid by adults. Also introduce the concepts of insurance and taxes. Make sure you take your child's level of maturity into account more than their age. If possible, either give your child access to the family budget, so they can see much is needed to run a household, or have them create their own budget with your help. Having a budget for their pocket-money, where they have to save up money for an item they want to buy, put aside money for Christmas gifts and (symbolically) paying for food can be very helpful in teaching them to account for expenses throughout the month and year later in life. Once again, cash is a very valuable tool for teaching, as it is a visual and physical form of currency, rather than digital, which can be very vague and difficult for us to visualize as something concrete.

Even as an adult, I still prefer cash as a method of controlling my day-to-day spending, both when it comes to groceries and my "allowance". Having control of my spending when it is solely digital is very difficult, and it is simplified greatly with cash. When I can physically see and feel how much is left, it is no longer vague, and I am able to pace the spending on daily living expenses much better.

Extreme generosity
While people with ASD have a very firm grasp the concept of personal property, they are also likely to be very generous, especially with money. As children and adolescents, they are likely to invite friends to the movies and to cafés in order to please and maintain friendships, without realizing how much they are spending, and without considering whether these friends ever do these things in return.

If someone asks for a loan for food or a bus ticket, your child is more likely than the neurotypical child to simply grant the loan without considering whether this person is ever going to pay them back, or if this person is even a friend of theirs.

Your child is also likely, due to this naivety, to fall for scams. Anything that promises a payback – like the scam emails that say you have inherited and you will be paid after you give a certain amount of money, or anything that threatens bad consequences, like the ones that say you have committed a crime and have to pay a fine. They are also likely to play the lottery or to gamble, honestly believing that at some point it will be their turn to win, because the concept of odds is either something we either understand very well, or not at all.

As your child grows older, talk about each of these things and what to do and why. It is important to teach them to protect themselves, without teaching them to be overly skeptical of people's intentions. You do not want to teach them to have negative expectations of everyone, just to keep their guard up against predators and scams. You also want them to know, that it is perfectly okay to want to do something nice for your friends, but to know the difference between when it is your own idea to do something and when friends might be trying to coerce you to do something.

Spending on special interests
This is something that can truly get out of hand. Even for the financially

aware individual, they can get caught up in their interest and wanting something so much for it that they cannot stop themselves. Some adults with ASD have wound up in immense debts because their spending on special interests was so out of proportion with their actual financial situation.

When it comes to the special interest, there can also be a strong lack of priorities. They may stay within budget, but not prioritize in healthy ways, sometimes opting for only one meal per day, or consciously spending less money on water, electricity, insurance or health care in favor of having more money for their interest. This is one of the reasons why it is so important to teach the concept of money and its value early on, and to train awareness of it as a skill. The point is not to encourage them to never spend, but to find the balance between wishes and reality. Unfortunately, while rare, there are cases where people with ASD will actually begin stealing from others in order to finance their interest. This may happen when they have no other options left within their own economy and because the special interest can become such an obsession that nothing else matters. If you see signs of this, I would advise to contact a specialist about this problem particularly. Even if you think it is expensive, or it is money you do not have, I would argue that once this spiral begins, the cost of almost any amount of therapy will pale in comparison to the fortune that can be spent and the troubles that can result from this sort of behavior. Get help sooner rather than later, and again, educate your child or adolescent as much as possible about money as early as possible, and encourage rational thinking when it comes to this aspect of life.

There is also the flip-side, where lack of control of every-day spending means that you cannot afford the things you want the most. Signe, a woman with Asperger's, wrote to me:

"I've probably always been good at spending money. On the other hand, I've also always tried to avoid it. It just never worked. Oddly, it's made my way of spending money very backwards. I have a hard time spending on things I really want, that have to do with my interests, probably because it is usually more expensive things, but small things I can spend lots of money on, as long as they are small amounts." (Signe, personal communication)

This is something that can make us profoundly miserable if we do not have humor about it. Once again, I suggest cash as a way of controlling spending. Self-irony can also alleviate the situation, if not financially, then emotionally.

Money as a special interest

This can be (almost) just as harmful as overspending. Once again, food, electricity and heat will be ignored in favor of the interest, but in this case, the interest is saving and keeping money. Think of it as collecting money rather than stamps.

The behavior will be scrooge-like. They will always go for the cheapest option and never buy anything they do not need. And when I say need, I may need as in "for survival"-need. This may come in varying degrees of severity, but in the most severe end, we are talking about a behavior where they will rather be wearing six shirts and cover themselves with blankets than they will turn on the heat. Of course, their bank-statement will look absolutely beautiful, but their life will not be. Again, seek out a specialist and encourage rational thinking and balance. You may want to settle for being happy with slightly less rational behavior than you would otherwise be. Focus on getting them to a point where their lives are reasonably comfortable and they are living in a healthy way, that is, convince them to at least turn on the heat. Try to teach them early on about the social consequences one will face from not sharing with others. This can be done through roleplaying and social stories.

Some people with ASD have a naturally healthy understanding of and attitude towards money which enables them to have great control of their finances and build their own fortune from a young age. They can be good at investing (and they are likely to put great effort into educating themselves and researching each investment), and they are likely to turn it into a career. In this case, I would put more energy into encouraging charity and empathy, as this is more likely to be the difficulty they face in life.

Entitlement
This problem is related to black and white thinking, and language. If your child is used to getting x pocket-money every week or month, and your situation changes so that the amount has to decrease, your child could well react with a sense of entitlement. Basically a "I have always gotten x amount of pocket-money, so I am supposed to get x amount of pocket-money" type of mind-frame. Here it is not so much rational thinking that causes the problem, rather it is lack of nuanced thinking. It is best to prepare the child for the change a good while in advance, and talk to them in an age-appropriate way about why there will be a change.

SIBLINGS

I do not have any myself, but many of us do, and many professionals make a point of speaking to both the children with ASD and non-ASD siblings. This chapter is based on information and ideas I have gathered through such channels. Because more trouble tends to occur when there are siblings of different neurology, rather than when both/all children either do or do not have ASD, I will be discussing the former situation in this chapter. So, when one child has ASD and another does not, what should you be aware of as a parent?

The safest child that is not me
Other children are strange and confusing and it is hard to get to know them. But a sibling is someone you watch every day as you both grow up. Therefore, a sibling will, for better or worse, be the child you know the best, after yourself. For a child with ASD that almost by default means it is the safest child to be around, simply because we know what to expect. Use this familiarity to create positive bonds between them. Depending on the age gap and who is older, you can either have the neurotypical child become a defender and a spokesperson, or the child without ASD become a teacher's assistant with you being the lead teacher, and in either case, give both children a sense of safety and pride about being kind and supportive to one another. I know, easier said than done. A young girl with Asperger's told me of her adult siblings:

"I feel safe with my siblings, and they help me with things. They are adult and moved out from home, but whenever they come to visit, we talk and play games together." (Anonymous, personal communication.)

So even with a big age gap, the older siblings can help to create a positive social environment. And the older the other children are, the more likely the young child with ASD will see them as role models and feel safe to ask them for help.

Why do they not understand me?
With siblings it can always go two ways. The child with ASD may wonder why their sibling does not understand their quirks or why they do not share their interests. Likewise, the neurotypical child may wonder why their sibling does not understand why certain things are annoying or important. And this confusion becomes greater because it is a sibling; it is a child that is so close, who has seen and shared many experiences, but who may still not understand very important things about the other.

Children with ASD can feel very confused about why their neurotypical sibling does not want to play the same games – and again, vice versa. Why do you, or do you not, think that this Lego collection is the greatest thing in the world!? So as a parent, you want to encourage them to play together, and help them find ways to do this. You also want to encourage and help them to understand each other where this is difficult.

The special needs taking priority
This is, once again, cause for confusion. Especially on the part of the neurotypical child. Why does my sibling get to eat certain things or, as might more often be the case, get to not eat certain things? Why does their sound sensitivity have to affect my play?

Of course, as the children get older, many things become easier to understand. But one effect of focusing on the needs of the child with ASD, is that this child will not get to see you, in an obvious, tangible way, taking their neurotypical sibling's needs into account to the same degree that their own needs are taken into account, and because of this they may have a harder time understanding their sibling's needs.

Because of that, and for exercises in empathy, make sure that you talk to the children (both together and separately) about how to make their sibling's lives easier, and congratulate them and compliment them when they do things for each other and for you. This also encourages a value system where other people's needs are prioritized, for both children with and without ASD.

Another possible problem are that the neurotypical child can feel overlooked. If your child with ASD has special teachers or assistants, or possibly a nanny with knowledge of the spectrum, your other child can get a feeling of "Why does he/she have an adult to themselves?", especially if that child is still very young.

Make sure you arrange for alone-time with both parents for both children to make sure they each are getting personal attention at some point. It may seem obvious when it is put in writing, but the more troubled one child is, the more the other can often be left to themselves, and while most find coping skills, it is still something to keep in mind.

Different rules for different children
There are usually different rules, also because of age. An older child is allowed to do other things than a younger one. But when the differences are because of something other than age, they are a little harder to explain and understand. And for young children, it is very hard to understand what it means that your sibling has ASD and needs different things than you do.

Fortunately, children are not prejudiced by nature, so an honest explanation, simplified to suit age, is a good place to start. They do, however, have a sense of justice which means that reasoning has to be fair. If you are explaining something to the child with ASD, it also has to follow ASD-logic, which can be trickier.

The other really tricky part is making the explanation age-appropriate. For example, it is very hard to explain to a young child that their sibling eats the same thing for dinner every night because you are doing your best to prevent a meltdown caused by sensory overload. Depending on the sibling's age, you could try things like: "He/she is the sort of person who prefers to eat the same thing for dinner every day" or "...gets scared when things are different than usual".

Especially when dealing with young children, I recommend avoiding language that makes it seem like an illness or disorder. This can cause several problems both in communication but also view of each other and oneself. You do not want one sibling to view the other as ill or wrong, but rather as different. You especially do not want the child with ASD to view themselves as ill or wrong. Therefore, try to find language that is neutral. Hence "the sort of person who..."

This leads to another, slightly connected, issue, which is a tendency to praise different children for different things, and in different amounts for the same things. This is not necessarily a bad thing, but when it is audible to both children, make sure they both get the high-five for having put on their pajamas correctly. Just as importantly, make sure that both high-fives are equally enthusiastic and honest. It may be that the younger neurotypical child has done it perfectly every evening for the last year or two and that this is the first time your child with ASD did it correctly/without complaint/the first time you said to/whatever else has been the problem – but if both children can hear and/or see the first high-five and "Good job!", they both get one. Again, it might seem obvious in writing, but in practice, it can easily be forgotten.

You embarrass me but I still defend you
Children who have siblings on the spectrum can have very ambivalent feelings towards them. On the one hand, they can be embarrassed when their sibling does something in public or in front of friends that is not quite normal. It is frustrating to have a sibling who has been making the same noise, or playing the same song, for the last hour, no matter how much you know they are fascinated by it. On the other hand, they are also the first to defend their siblings when others stare or ridicule.

It is okay to feel embarrassed. It is not the reaction one wishes they had, but it is there and it is how they feel. That is okay. It is not okay to voice it in a patronizing manner or in public, but it is okay to feel it. It is also okay to feel frustrated. It is okay to feel angry at times.

If you see them react to someone staring or perhaps even saying something back, for example; "It's rude to stare at someone else like that. He/she can't help being who he/she is." make sure you encourage this and reinforce standing up for your sibling as a good thing and that defending them makes you a good sister or brother. Acknowledge their feelings, and encourage them to defend their sibling, no matter who is older and who is younger.

Flaws are easy to see

Anyone can probably name something annoying about a family member they live with. Flaws or frustrating characteristics are easy to notice and easy to remember. And when children go to school and generally into the world, there will be no shortage of people who can tell them what they are not good at.

So an exercise, once again in empathy but also in bonding, is talking about the things each child is good at and likes to do. One might really like to sing or to memorize lyrics, one might like a certain computer game. One could be really good at spelling or coming up with stories, one might be good at imitating voices or drawing.

Encourage the children to notice what their sibling likes to do and what they are good at, and encourage them to complement each other from time to time (the child with ASD might need to know exactly how often to do so, or need extra prompting, but may also overdo it) – either way, it is something to work on and with.

LISTS, SCHEDULES AND REMINDERS

As a parent, you are going to be doing a lot of listing, scheduling and reminding, in the effort to lessen anxiety and satisfy the need for structure and sameness. Having a little control of your world in the form of predictability can go a long way towards our emotional stability, and is therefore doing a big part of preventing meltdowns.

"The world is absolutely draining and overwhelming. Schedules and routines are one of the only ways for me to keep order in a disorderly world. Routines in my daily life gives me control in a way I don't get elsewhere and knowing how and when something is happening, in the form of a schedule, minimizes the chance of a meltdown because of an unforeseen event. It takes my brain a long time to adapt. So even if a situation is stressing and uncomfortable, just knowing about it in details beforehand, can make it bearable." (Ellen, personal communication.)

Schedules, schedules for everything

Your child is given a schedule for school, but it is not complete. You may want to make your own print-out schedule for each day, making sure you child has information which classes and where, but which teacher. You want to fill in whether they take a bus or train to and from school or if they are being brought and picked up. What is for lunch? The more information your child has ahead of the day, the easier it is to get through.

For evenings and weekends, it is more of a judgement call. Does your child feel comfortable not having a schedule at home? Do they maybe need unscheduled time? If you do have a schedule at home, and it says dinner at 6pm, then dinner may have to be at 6pm exactly depending on your child's profile. But really, when it comes to being in a safe place, which home is, some children on the spectrum function very well without schedules, so try it out and find what suits your child best.

For extracurricular activities, playdates and family get-togethers, there should be some amount of schedule as well, especially if your child is feeling anxious or stressed. It should specify when you are leaving home, when you are supposed to arrive, estimates for what times meals will take place, estimates for what time you are going home etc. Again, all depending on how detailed your child needs it to be – some children need very little, others need everything specified.

Your child's need for schedules may also very well change as they grow older. There can also be sudden changes in times of anxiety, depression and stress.

Rituals, routine and hygiene

There can be quite many rituals, often made by the child themselves. Certain things can have a touch of OCD to them – but do not worry unless it controls their lives. You probably also have a certain order in your morning ritual, and you probably do not even think about it.

They may want the cereal box in a specific place on the table, or want to wear or not to wear certain colors together, even without this having a basis in sensory sensitivities. It is just a little thing that makes them feel good to do a certain way.

However, other routines and rituals may have to be established by you. For example, providing the order and checklist for dressing oneself. Remembering to check which way the shirt goes, and how to identify this, etc.

They may also need a routine/checklist in the shower. They may very well forget the body wash or shampoo, and so this needs to be established early on. Some sort of ritual which can become more and more well-practiced so they will eventually, hopefully, no longer have to think about every little thing.

One very important point has to do with dental hygiene. It is very common to have sensory sensitivities with regard to our teeth and gums. Many of us have rather extreme dislike towards brushing teeth either for that reason, or because we hate the taste of toothpaste.

Dentists advise that parents check their children's tooth brushing, or even redo it after every time, up to around age twelve. But your child has ASD. You do not stop at age twelve. Until your child has caught up in terms of executive functions to the extent that they can remember and do this correctly every time, you do not stop.

I stress this point because some children have been known to simply stop brushing their teeth once their parents stop checking, and once the routine drops, they do not pick it up again. So your child could suddenly decide at age 15 or 16, when you think that now, surely, they can manage themselves, to stop brushing their teeth because they do not like it, and a few years later, you start seeing the evidence.

So any ritual or routine that has to do with something your child does not like doing, should be checked, especially when it has to do with their well-being.

For as long as it is possible, try to make it a calm social activity to, for example, brush your teeth together in the mornings and evenings. Once the child becomes older and perhaps does not find it fun to do together anymore, find some way of checking it without intruding too much on their sense of self. Perhaps there are apps or electric toothbrushes that record how long one spent brushing one's teeth. Do some research and see what is available in your country.

Lists

Lists are especially useful to combat our problems with planning and prioritizing. As a young child, I used to have meltdowns at the mere request that I tidy my room. It was not that I did not want to tidy my room, it was that I had no idea where to start, where to end, or to what standards it should be tidied. Lists help incredibly. Even now, as an adult, I make a list of what needs doing when I can no longer distinguish beginning from end. Then, when I am done with everything on the list, I can see if anything else needs doing.

While your child is young they will need you to compile the lists, but as they grow older you can include them in the process, thereby teaching them a skill they will need throughout their whole lives.

Reminders

Even with all of these lists and schedules, we still need reminders sometimes. And it is hard to find a balance between reminding your child too many times, and too few. You know your child best, but try to remember that their needs and abilities change (and hopefully improve) as they get older, so when at age seven, they might need ten reminders leading up to an event, they might need four by the time they are twelve. Or they might need one.

Due to the individual nature of autism and its expression, it is very hard to predict correctly what sort of maturing and learning curve you will have to deal with. But to the extent that it is possible, you should try to adapt to it. A good place to begin implementing reminders is if there is a major event coming up. Give the first reminder a week ahead, then five days before, three days, two days, one day before. The reminders should not be big or dramatic in any way; they should be calm reminders. They should also preferably be visual, so if you can, possibly have a calendar hanging somewhere in easy height for your child, and with them, cross out each day leading up to a major event. They may also enjoy crossing the days out every day, in which case you can do this with them, and then calmly remind them when there is a certain number of days to an event. Such a calendar can also be color coded. I find that color coding works very well because of our visual way of thinking. Let your child choose which color school should be, which color for an activity, playdates, family events and so on and so forth. Then have pens in each of those colors close by so that they are ready for adding things to the calendar.

SELF-IDENTITY

Who am I?

When your behavior mimics that of others to the extent that it does for some children on the spectrum; it can become quite difficult to discern who you are from the person or persons you mimic. This is especially true for girls, as they are more prone to using that form of social adaptation. We can begin to question if we like the things we do because they like them, or because we like them. Do I wear the same clothes because it is pretty or because I am trying to be normal? This usually does not last for many years, but it ends up taking a lot of time and energy to deal with nonetheless.

What you can do as a parent is to point out aspects of their personality and preferences from an early age, and discuss how these are good things. The idea is not forcing a certain identity on your child, or to force them away from the identity of the children and adults they mimic, but rather to instill confidence in your child that who they are, even if they adapt to social situations differently depending on where they are, is someone who is loved, appreciated and who has good values and characteristics.

With confidence should eventually come the ability to shed some of the mask and march to their own beat.

Sexual identity and vulnerability

Children and adolescents with ASD develop hormonally at the same pace as neurotypicals, but accompanied by a delayed emotional maturity. This can cause some issues, in terms of identity and vulnerability.

Usually, a problem arises when the children and adolescents around them begin developing their sexual identities and their behavior begins to change. Different clothes are expected if you want to be cool, and peer pressure can take on new forms. Suddenly, everyone else is saying that they have already had their first kiss, others will claim to have done more, and because of your child's naivety, they will believe these things as true without question and think that this behavior is expected of them, much earlier than other children, in some cases. This leads directly into the main point, which is vulnerability. As with bullying, we have no radar to spot predators. We also may not realize that it is okay to say no.

What usually happens is that we can very easily be overwhelmed by positive attention once someone gives it to us, and that we will do almost anything to maintain it. We are easily manipulated, especially because we will not always say no even when we want to scream and run. Thus, we are more likely to end up in situations where we cannot escape, and therefore, as a demographic, we are vulnerable to being sexually assaulted or even raped.

I do not mention this to scare you. You should not lock your child or adolescent up for the rest of their lives. Again it comes down to confidence. Teach us that it is okay to say no, and teach us that this is the strong and smart thing to do. When your child reaches the age where others begin dating, or if your child's body matures early, begin teaching them how not to wind up in situations without the possibility of escape. Teach them never to go off with a stranger, but instead to call someone they know and be picked up, or to call a taxi and tell them you will pay because otherwise, they might think they cannot afford this escape route. Teach them to give the wrong phone number if they need to get rid of someone – yes, teach them to lie! Things that may seem obvious to you will not occur to your child.

Gender identity and sexual orientation

Another and rarer problem in this category, is that if your child has a tendency to mimic others, they may choose social groups and even sexual orientations to mimic, taking it on as a part of their identity. This is usually a "Hey, those people are also not accepted by the mainstream so I'll just be one of them!"-reaction. This goes back to the earlier point about giving them confidence in who they are. Also, like neurotypical adolescents, figuring out who you are is a learning curve, so they may figure out later that this is not them.

But for the most part, if your child tells you they are gay, bi-sexual, asexual or any other sexuality, it is probably because they have done their research and truly feel this way.

A young teenage girl with Asperger's explains:

"I think I am bi-sexual. I know it's normal to experiment during the teenage years, but it doesn't feel like a phase when I have feelings for a girl. I also talk to the boys in class about girls and stuff."

"My mum always 'joked' that she wouldn't be surprised if I came out as gay or bi-sexual at some point, so I always felt safe about it. I've been quite sure of my sexuality since I was 12 years old. A lot of my friends are a little older than me, and almost all of them are homo-, bi- or pansexual." (Anonymous, personal communication.)

Being quite young as she is, I find it remarkable that she even knows the term pansexual, but this is what I mean when I say they usually do their research.

In people with ASD there is a larger proportion of the population, relative to the general population, who are not cisgender (someone whose gender corresponds to the sex assigned at birth) and/or heterosexual. That is, a larger percentage of us feel and identify as a different gender than the body we were born with, and a larger percentage are not attracted to the opposite gender, or at least not only to the opposite gender.

The proportion of asexuality is also much higher than in the general population. Being asexual is very different from being celibate. If you are celibate, you have sexual attractions but do not act on them, whereas someone who is an asexual has no desire to be sexually active with anyone, though many still want life partners.

I include this to let you know that any of these thoughts and ideas should be taken seriously. Once they come and tell you, you should assume that they probably know what they are talking about, and have thought about it a great deal, and therefore you should do your best to react in a neutral or positive manner. Reacting in a negative way can have serious, long term consequences for your relationship, and for the self-esteem and self-worth of your child.

HOMEWORK

There are so many of aspects that make homework a challenge for people with ASD. We learn differently, perceive differently and we think differently, so therefore we do not always understand the problems we are supposed to solve, or we may not interpret them in the same way as they are intended.

Handwriting

Some ASD children will find it quite easy. These are often the ones who also have skills in drawing and painting. However, due to the general tendency toward fine motor skill problems, handwriting can be a serious issue. Holding a pencil and making our hands create letters can be incredibly frustrating, and much more so because it is often combined with a need for perfection. So having to learn to write at a young age is likely to be a grueling task, filled with tears and meltdowns.

The solution to this is rather simple, if the school is willing to cooperate. Allow your child to type instead. Let them focus on solving the written assignment rather than being endlessly frustrated at their own handwriting. It is not a productive use of energy or time if your child becomes so sad about their handwriting that they cannot complete their assignments, and hopefully the teachers and school can see this.

Distractions

The environment needed to get through homework is usually rather Spartan. You will want to eliminate as many sensory distractions as possible, consider both desk and chair, light, sound, temperature and smells. Make this an environment that is focused only on the task ahead.

If you have the room for it, try having a specific desk only for homework, so that in your child's mind, there is no other activity that can be indulged in at this desk. They should not be distracted by thoughts of drawings, or their colored pencils being right next to them.

Asking for help

This is something that is difficult for us to remember as a possibility.

When we are trying to solve a problem, we are so focused on that task and on trying to shove away the feeling of frustration that comes from not succeeding, that we forget to even consider that someone else may have the answer. It is simply not a natural course of action for us.

Another problem is that we may not even realize when help is needed. For example, many written assignments are phrased by the teacher to mean one thing, but we, being literal thinkers, understand it quite differently. So we end up solving a different task from the one that was set. And we have no clue that we are actually in need of assistance, because we do not know to check for such misunderstandings.

So your job, and the teachers' job, is to introduce the concepts of asking for and receiving help, and making this a positive experience. You can do this through setting up short and simple roleplaying games or writing Social Stories about asking for help, receiving it and the problem being solved. These should also include how to ask for help politely and thanking the person who provided help.

After this, you must make sure to make help available, and to inform teachers of how you have instructed your child in asking for help, and make them aware of how important it is that your child has good experiences asking for and receiving help at school.

Learning styles

There is a lot of debate about learning styles and how to apply them, and some even question if there is such a thing. The fact is that people on the spectrum tend to be very visual thinkers, and generally, the track record for learning and retaining information provided visually to us, in the form of images, not text, far surpasses that of being taught through audio or text only.

However, we are all different, so do not take this as the end-all-be-all. This is merely a suggestion to look more closely at how your child learns best, and to adapt to that as much as possible.

If we have to remember a story for a school discussion, we may remember it much better if you act it out together with figures on a table, or if you make drawings of key scenes.

So look into it, try your way ahead, and communicate with teachers to find the best way for your child to learn and retain knowledge.

Mistakes

As mentioned in the section about handwriting, there can be a great deal of perfectionism and therefore also frustration when mistakes are made. In terms of handwriting, a letter not being shaped perfectly can either cause a meltdown, or will prompt us to erase and redo it until it is perfect.

If a mistake is made in a report and marked in red by the teacher, the reaction can be very dramatic because to us, that red mark does not mean we made a mistake; it means we are stupid, and that everything about that report is bad and wrong. This is black and white thinking; it is lack of nuance. Making mistakes make us feel as if it is the end of the world, and that nothing can ever fix it again, because we cannot take back that mistake.

What we need, is to develop a positive view of mistakes. This takes a very long time to learn, but in my view, it is also one of the most important skills for us to learn because everyone will keep making mistakes all through their lives. There is always going to be one more.

Again, take up the wonderful world of roleplaying games and Social Stories. Create stories and games exploring someone making a mistake and learning from it. Talk to your child about how sometimes, people make the same mistake many times before they have learned to correct it, but it does not matter how long it takes, as long as you try your best.

Encourage the view that it is okay to be wrong, and it is smart to admit when you are wrong and being open to changing opinions based on facts and evidence; that this does not make you stupid, but, in fact, shows how smart and mature you are. Do not expect this to take hold quickly. It goes against our natural inclinations. But after some years, you may have helped your child to develop the skill to accept and even appreciate mistakes as learning experiences.

Time scale

The last point I want to make about homework is one about time scale. When a teacher sets an assignment, they usually have an idea of how long this task is supposed to take. But your child, with their way of thinking, their perfectionism and their exhaustion after a school day, will be likely to spend much more time and energy on each task than intended by the teacher.

Talk to your child's teachers about setting a time scale on each homework assignment. An estimate on how long they think it should take. It could be 30 minutes or two hours, but if the teacher takes two seconds to write that on the piece of paper they hand to your child, then you know that the assignment is not supposed to take half the night. Your child should not be struggling to get through homework assignments for three times as long as was intended. They need and deserve time off.

So with a time estimate on each assignment, you know to tell your child: "You will be spending 30 minutes on this one, and if you are not done, that is okay."

They will have put in the time and energy, but they also still need time to relax and recover from the day because the complete and utter exhaustion from a school day is something most people with ASD have experienced. A young woman with Asperger's, Signe, wrote to me about the exhaustion from school:

"I never did my homework. I did only what I had to hand in, but only just. I sat down for an hour or two and typed away, not even bothering to spell-check. I did just fine in school anyway. I was so tired and run down after school that I would just sit in the living room and watch TV until my parents came home, and then I would go to my room and read." (Signe, personal communication.)

ANIMALS

Most people with ASD respond very well to having animals around them, and many even express liking animals better than people. This is probably because animals are much less complicated and unpredictable in their behavior than people are. They can become a life-long special interest and a career, and they can be instrumental at reducing stress and anxiety.

In the countries where therapy animals can be given to children with ASD, many gain enormous benefit from having a therapy dog or cat. But it is important to note that it is not just dogs and cats that can be therapeutically beneficial for a child with ASD.

Learning empathy and Theory of Mind

Animals in general, but especially mammals, are a great introduction to learning the skills in empathy and Theory of Mind that are lacking, namely, understanding the emotions of others and pinpointing where the emotion originates from.

With an animal such as a cat or dog, it is rather easy to tell if they are happy, excited, angry, scared, tired, surprised and so on. And even if your child is in the severe end of ASD in terms of lacking skills within empathy, such animals provide an easy introduction to emotions and their origins. The dog is happy because you came home from school, it missed you. The dog is anxious because you are taking its bone away, and it really likes the bone and wants it back. When you are sad, very often a cat or dog will attempt to comfort you (other mammals will do this, too) even though it does not know why you are sad. This provides an avenue for you to talk with your child about how the animal knew they were sad, and how it tried to comfort them, even though it did not know or understand why they were sad.

There is also an easy introduction to Theory of Mind, in that the dog has to learn tricks; it does not magically know what you want it to do. Its behavior is relatively easy to predict and the spectrum of emotional reactions is less nuanced (as far as we know), and therefore easier to deal with as a concept.

Care-taking

Another concept that is learnt in practical ways is care-taking. This is most especially true if your child is around very young animals, or even assists in breeding. I personally grew up with a dog kennel. We had new puppies to take care of fairly often, and since I could crawl, I have been involved in taking care of puppies from they were born until they were around eight weeks old, as well as the adult dogs.

This taught me about care-taking in a very concrete manner. For example, the puppies had to all be weighed every day. Why? To make sure they were gaining weight. Why? Because this would mean they were eating and growing as they should.

I helped to clean up their business, because this has to be done to make sure their living environment is healthy. And so the list goes. There were good and logical reasons for doing everything that needed doing in regard to both puppies and adults. I helped cut their nails, brush them, teach them cleanliness, socialize with them and exercise them, mostly running around the lawn in my case, due to my aversion to being in public.

This all taught me about basic needs and fulfilling them, not in order to satisfy myself, but to take care of another living being.

In learning this, you also learn to postpone your own needs in favor of the needs of the pet's needs. It cannot wait an hour to take a walk, because it has to go now. It needs your attention, your care, your time, which means you have to learn how to fulfill that need while temporarily ignoring your own. Your child will need your guidance to learn this, just as a neurotypical child will.

I am sure that learning these skills can also be achieved through helping with a baby, provided your child is old enough when the baby arrives. In learning these skills, what matters are the logical reasons to do things, combined with this next point.

Building connections

You build a connection with this living being that is in your care. You learn slowly, over time, what makes them happy, excited and playful, and what makes them relax. They reciprocate in ways that are easy to understand, given a little education about the animal. A cat bumping you with its head, or a dog bringing you a toy when you are sad, sleeping in bed with you or curling up at your feet; either protecting you or being protected, feeling safe. Slowly, a relationship builds and what is very much a friendship emerges.

For a child who is stressed out from trying to deal with people, their emotions and language, their unfathomable reasons for doing things, and their frustrating, constant urge to speak, it is a considerable relief to be able to snuggle up on the couch and have your animal join you silently, asking for nothing from you. Likewise, it is a relief to have that animal come and want to play, because at least you know how to play this game, and you know how to tell if the animal is happy with you or not.

This is a safe friend, one who will never betray you, one that is always happy to see you. It is one that seems to understand you when no one else does, because they do not question your emotions or ask anything of you when you have nothing left to give. They support you just as you support them. In this way, the reciprocity of a friendship with an animal is very simple and easy to grasp for a child with ASD.

All in all, though sometimes it is a chore to walk your dog at 5am in the rain or snow, the benefits of having an animal around are incredible and invaluable.

For many people on the spectrum, animals are great company, very often preferred to that of humans, because it is company we can bear.

"To be honest, I probably like animals more than humans. I'm a vegetarian, an animal rights activist (when I have energy for it) and I want to be a vet after school. I've loved animals for as long as I can remember and they never cease, no matter if it's a spider or puppy, to put a smile on my face. I think it's because animals are a lot easier to understand than humans. People are so difficult to read and comprehend, while animals are honest and they do not judge you like people do. That's my kind of company." (Ellen, personal communication.)

WHAT HELPS IN THE BIG PICTURE?

There are "big fixes" in life. I am not talking about "curing" all of our problems, but rather, increasing overall physical and mental health. These "fixes" aren't things you learn to use effectively on your own until adulthood, if at all, which is why I want to tell you, the parents. When speaking to people with ASD about what helps them in the bigger picture, it is very often the same things you will hear. I hope that some children will reap the benefits earlier in life, and that this can assist in laying the foundation for a happy and successful life.

So, what really helps?

Regular sleep and daylight

Most of us have trouble with sleep. Generally, what I hear, as well as experience myself, is that our minds wake up at night. Unfortunately, society does not agree with that. However, because it is so easy for us to be awake at night, and we get our best work done after sundown, it is essential that we have regular sleeping patterns, and that our sleep is as good as possible. Getting enough daylight is really good for the brain and helps the brain maintain a regular sleeping pattern. The rhythm of daylight tells the brain when it is time to wake up, and when it is time to sleep. Giving your brain these cues for a day-rhythm goes a long way!

There are a few tools available. It is not enough to simply have a routine with set sleeping hours, that do not change during the weekend, along with getting plenty of daylight, you can try one or several of these options:

- Taking extra vitamin D. Many of us are vitamin D deficient, and taking some extra can help tremendously. Be aware that some people may have to take this along with calcium – ask the doctor.

- Weighted blankets/duvets. Adults with ASD have told me how these help them to gather themselves mentally, and helps increase awareness of their body, providing a sense of being grounded and safe. They are especially good for those who have problems with the proprioceptive sense. There are duvets and blankets available with different forms of weight in them. Some are noisier than others, and some are heavier than others. See if this can be a solution. Many people with ASD speak very highly of these, although some note that they sometimes have to change the weight. I know that some people keep two of them with different weight, and change between the two according to their need.

- Melatonin. I would only recommend taking extra melatonin during periods of difficulty falling asleep. Melatonin is not a conventional sleeping pill, but is more of a sleep regulator, mostly used in circadian rhythm disorders. Circadian rhythm disorders are when a person is unable to sleep and wake at the normal times required for school, work and social needs. These types of disorders are common in people with ASD, though it is not known exactly why. Melatonin is one of the treatments used for these types of disorders. Melatonin is only proven to have a moderate effect in patients above the age of 55. This could mean either that the effect described by so many on the spectrum is the result of a placebo effect, or we generally react differently to it than the general population, and there simply are no studies to show this. I cannot tell you which it is, I can only tell you my experience, and what I have heard from others on the spectrum. My experience is that it helps me to fall asleep. It does not keep me asleep however, but also does not inhibit dreaming. I, personally, use it, after consultation with my doctor, to restore a regular sleeping pattern when nothing else works, yet before considering "normal" sleeping pills, because my problem is never insomnia but a circadian rhythm one. I do know that some take it daily, but these are relatively rare cases, as far as I know, and I would not recommend this without explicit permission and regular follow-up consultations with your doctor. When it comes to this option, always consult your doctor, and maintain a conversation about it whenever there are changes. More research is needed in this field.

The following two "big fixes" also play a major role in a good sleeping pattern, and I would avoid medication before trying these.

Good, nutritious diet
It is an annoying cliché, yet you never escape it. And when you have sensory sensitivities concerning food, it can be extra annoying listening to people telling you to "eat right". But it works.

The fact is that there is no diet that is a cure-all. Some people swear by eating gluten-free, but for others it makes no difference at all. I stress this point because most people on the spectrum reap no benefit from limiting their diets in this way. My point is not to tell you to avoid certain things, or to eat a lot of something specific. I am not advocating any particular diet. What I am advocating, is a normal, balanced diet. Everything in moderation, as they say. Try to find ways to make fruits and vegetables appealing to your child. They do not have to like every type of meat, or like meat at all, but it is important to get enough protein, and so on and so forth. Where it is impossible to get them to eat something, for example fish, see if a supplement is available and needed. Again, consult your family doctor. They can take blood tests that show if your child has any vitamin deficiency. You do not have to make your child or household fanatically healthy, just healthy enough. You do not have to cut sugar, carbs, gluten or anything else. Just aim for a regular balanced diet, with regular meals and snacks.

Exercise
Again, a really annoying cliché that actually works. Note that exercise does not necessarily mean running. There are console games that can track movement, in which you can virtually play tennis, bowling, do yoga and many, many other things. Walking is an option. Playing with your dog can be exercise, depending on how you do it. Dancing, swimming, climbing... anything.

But the fact is, regular exercise is good for you. It is not only good for your heart, your other muscles, your blood flow and all that, it is also good for your brain. It releases endorphins, which makes you feel good, and can therefore help manage and reduce depressions. Furthermore, it can also help make you tired for the night, which means your sleep is less likely to be restless and disturbed.

A support system
There will never be a lack of people telling us what we cannot do, what we are bad at and how we are wrong, and there is only one antidote to constantly being told you are wrong, which is also constantly being told you are good, and that you belong.

We, like everybody else, need people around us who appreciate us and who tell us when we do something right. And because we so often make social mistakes which are so often pointed out to us in hurtful ways, we need a little extra awesome in our lives. You and our friends is the source for that awesome. We need you to tell us when we get things right and to give us the, perhaps not physical, high-five when this happens. We need you to be there for us, ready to talk when we finally find the words, patient enough to wait. We need you to listen, we need you to catch us when we fall, and we need you to help us gather the courage to get back up. The importance of a supportive family and friends cannot be overstated. You can mean the difference between a life of depressions and not feeling worthy, and a happy, fulfilling and successful one.

However, sometimes we may need more than a social support system. For those of us who have trouble with comorbid disorders, we can be in need of a financial support system as well. This does not necessarily mean that you support us for our whole lives. What it means is that, for us, knowing that we do not have to worry about surviving can mean the difference between being able to function reasonably and being permanently crippled by the anxiety that if we make a single mistake it will all fall apart. So depending on who your child is and whether or not they have extra diagnoses, they may need either government support, or they may need to simply know that if it all goes to hell, you will make sure they can eat.

Acceptance
Nothing works without this.

We need you to be okay with our autism. We need you to love us, not in spite of it, but with it. Autism is not "the problem". We do not need to be cured.

What makes life hard for us, in the long run, is not having to compensate for sensory sensitivities, delayed theory of mind skills, impaired executive functions or having really weird interests. What *does* make life really hard is the people who require that we become like them in order to be accepted. Because we are not like them.

We are not neurotypical. We are autistic. Our experience and perception of the world is critically different from yours, and that is okay.

If you do not make it into a problem, and instead see our qualities and talents, your whole experience of autism will change, and our whole lives will change. You teach others how to look at us with the way you speak about us and autism, and with the way you react when people say things. Because it can be hard for your child to find the words, you are your child's advocate in this world. You are their voice until they find their own. When we do something not quite normal in public and a stranger says something, your response is absorbed in detail. Your response tells the stranger how to see us and it tells onlookers how to see us. It tells them how to see autism.

You also teach us how to look at ourselves. Not to feel wrong, but merely different. Not to feel worth less than another, but to feel as a human being of equal value. Not to feel ashamed when we are misunderstood, but simply to correct the misunderstanding. To dare to speak at all.

To accept our autism and be okay with who we are, and to feel that we deserve the same respect as anyone else.

This is why the most important thing you will ever teach your child, is to accept and appreciate their autism as a part of who they are.

REFERENCES

Attwood, T. (2007) The Complete Guide to Asperger's Syndrome. London: Jessica Kingsley Publishers.

Grandin, T. (1984) 'My experiences as an autistic child and review of selected literature.' Journal of Orthomolecular Psychiatry 13, 144-174.

Hadcroft, W. (2005) The Feeling's Unmutual: Growing Up with Asperger Syndrome (Undiagnosed). London: Jessica Kingsley Publishers.

Jackson, N. (2002) Standing Up Falling Down: Asperger's Syndrome from the Inside Out. Bristol: Lucky Duck Publishing.

Lawson, W. (2001) Understanding and Working with the Spectrum of Autism: An Insider's View. London: Jessica Kingsley Publishers.

Willey, L.H. (1999) Pretending to be Normal: Living with Asperger's Syndrome. London: Jessica Kingsley Publishers.

Williams, D. (1998) Nobody Nowhere: The Remarkable Autobiography of an Autistic Girl. London: Jessica Kingsley Publishers.

Printed in Great Britain
by Amazon